KNITTINGCOLOR

Design Inspiration from Around the World

KNITTINGCOLOR

Design Inspiration from Around the World

Brandon Mably

of the Kaffe Fassett Studio

sixth&spring books

sixth&spring
books

Editorial Director
Trisha Malcolm

Art Director
Chi Ling Moy

Graphic Designer
Sheena T. Paul

Book Division Manager
Erica Smith

Associate Editor
Erin Walsh

Yarn Editor
Tanis Gray

Workshop Editor
Sarah Hoggett

Instructions Writer
Sharon Brant

Instructions Editors
Pat Harste
Emily Harste

Instructions Proofreader
Rita Greenfeder

Technical Illustrations
Jennifer Howell
Uli Mönch
Frances Soohoo

Copy Editors
Wendy R. Preston
Kathy Edgar

Fashion Photography
Sheila Rock

Still Photography
Dan Howell

Fashion Stylist
Adina Klein

Assistant Fashion Stylist
Misty Gunn

Production Manager
David Joinnides

President and Publisher, Sixth&Spring Books
Art Joinnides

Library of Congress Control Number: 2006924834
ISBN 13: 978-1-933027-07-4
ISBN 10: 1-933027-07-X

Manufactured in China

3 5 7 9 10 8 6 4 2

First Edition

Table of Contents

Introduction by Kaffe Fassett

Soon after Brandon joined my studio as manager in 1991, he became curious to learn the various crafts I used in my work. He learned patchwork, needlepoint, mosaic, and rag rug making, but knitting posed the biggest challenge to him.

Being dyslexic, Brandon struggled with the mechanics of his first few swatches, but his fertile imagination was brimming with ideas by the time he mastered the techniques. He has an innate sense of style—the sort of talent one is definitely born with. Trained in catering, with no art experience, he had after one day in my studio a sense of what worked in a design and what diluted its potential.

Brandon's feeling for color and its mysterious power was always there to be developed. Rarely have I been around someone whose judgment is so sure when it comes to sorting out colors. Not tempted to imitate my customary layered style, he has carved out his own graphic, yet playful approach to design. His pared-down compositions attract even beginner knitters and help them overcome any fear of pattern or color they might have.

Long ago I turned my knit workshops over to Brandon when I saw how encouraging he was as a teacher. Every person seems to leave Brandon's class empowered to work in color and create his or her own look.

I can't help feeling that Brandon will pass that same sense of confidence on to the knitters who work from this book. He has carefully worked out the colors for each design on these pages, but I will be curious to see what personal colors others come up with to better suit themselves.

Photo: Debbie Patterson

Preface

Over the years as a knitwear designer, I've had the fortune of traveling to different parts of the world giving "Color in Design" workshops. In this book, I share with you some of the snapshots from my travels that have inspired my designs. All the garments are fairly straightforward to knit, using basic stockinette stitch along with a simple color technique I use. Once you get this under your belt, let the color do the work. This book pays homage to all the places I've been; it's also a visual travel diary for those who offered to "carry my bags" in envy of these adventures over the years.

I started my career in knitwear design in the early '90s when I turned from catering to working with yarns and colors. This unusual career change came about through an accidental meeting at a bus stop near my apartment in London, with the man who put color knitting on the map—Kaffe Fassett. The moment I first walked into Kaffe's studio, I was enthralled by the environment. Shelves were stacked high with spools of colored yarns in different textures, Oriental pots sat on layers of Kilim carpets, and paintings were hung between bookshelves covering every available inch of wall space. It felt like walking into a cavern collaged with treasures from every corner of the world. This was my first brush with this kaleidoscopic world of color and design, and I knew right away that I wanted to be a part of it.

I observed the running of the studio while watching Kaffe execute commissions and create the books he is now famous for. Asking for my input on the designs he was creating, and liking the intuitive answers I gave, he encouraged me to try designing myself. As I grew as a designer, I slowly took over the running of the studio and began teaching his workshops myself.

These teaching opportunities have taken me to every corner of the world—from the frozen landscape of Iceland to the sun-baked out-

back of Australia, from Asia and Africa to North and South America. And everything in these varied and exotic lands has stimulated my designer's eye. In this book, I want to share with you some of the fantastic places that have so inspired me with their unique color happenings. Through photographs taken on my various journeys, you will see the inspirations that have fed my creativity over the years: the vegetable market of Vietnam with its fabric decorated stalls stacked high with brightly colored fruit; the rice fields in the countryside; strings of beads and bracelets hanging up in stalls in India; woven blankets from the textile weavers of Peru; and the clear rich blues and off-whites of the awesome glaciers of Alaska.

I hope you will find a wide selection of garments and accessories throughout the book to entice you, along with suggestions on colorways. Feel free to adjust the shaping of the garments—turning a jacket into a sweater, perhaps adding sleeves to a vest, or translating any

design into a pillow. I am quite basic in my approach to knitting techniques, concentrating on using good old stockinette stitch and the intarsia and Fair Isle techniques described in detail in the back of the book.

I hope the journeys in this book interest you as much as they have interested me over the years.

Keep the colors flowing!

Brandon Mably

Color Workshop

All my work begins with color. I see it all around me—in the landscape, in buildings, in other artists' creations—and I'm always on the lookout for new, exciting combinations of shapes and textures that I can translate into a design.

Because I give workshops on color all over the world, many people assume I must have a theory, or even a magic formula for guaranteed success every time. If that's what you're hoping to find in the following pages, then I'm afraid you'll be sorely disappointed. The bad news is that, when it comes to color, there's no such thing as a magic formula! There are countless books on color theory that purport to hold all the answers, and learning about color theory certainly won't do you any harm—provided you're aware that it's only part of the story. But there's absolutely no substitute for hands-on experience.

One of the reasons color theory can let you down is that a simple color wheel, like the kind you see in art and design books, contains only twelve colors, whereas the human eye can discern hundreds, if not thousands, of different shades. Moreover, most of the color wheels you see reproduced in books are flat, mechanical pieces of artwork, often computer-generated—but when you're working with yarn (par-

ticularly natural fibers), you're dealing with texture and an infinite number of different shades. How can reading about color theory equip you to cope with that kind of subtlety?

Dealing with color in knitting—or any other medium, for that matter—is also a very personal process. Only you know what yarns you have at your disposal; only you can physically place one yarn next to another and assess how the colors work together; only you can assess your own emotional response to the color combinations you come up with. I don't believe anyone has the right to tell you that a particular combination of colors works, or doesn't work. If you like something, then it's right for you. (And even if you produce something that you don't like, someone else may fall head over heels in love with it!)

What I do with my students is get them to really look at the color they're using. It's much more challenging than simply reading about

the theory, but ultimately, I believe, it's also far more empowering: It equips you to translate what you see around you into a design. In my workshops I take my students through a three-stage process, which I'd like to share with you. Go through the same process in your own home—and then go through it again and again, until it becomes instinctive. Like every skill, it's a matter of practice.

Stage 1: Analyzing color combinations

I don't necessarily expect you to come up with winning color combinations right from the outset, so start by analyzing someone else's creation.

Find a postcard of a favorite painting and try to work out why it appeals to you. Gather balls of yarn in shades similar to those in the painting, and see if they create the same effect. You'll realize that the

From left to right: Hands pillows; schoolchildren's decorations on a waste can in South Africa; rice fields in Vietnam; Bali vest.

proportion of colors has a lot to do with their dynamic. You might notice how a large area of earthy browns is activated by purple or moss green, how lemons and tangerines can be brightened by a hint of a sharp lime tone. Observe the level of intensity of the color scheme by determining which tones are the darkest and lightest. Is there a pure white or a true black? Notice how multi-shades that are close together vibrate, and how a bold color can bring a bland group of colors to life. Most great paintings will reveal some truth about color that will enhance your own work. (If you're wondering why I suggest working from a painting rather than from a photograph, it's because a photograph always looks flatter than a painting. The subtleties, the transitions from one shade to another, tend to be evened out and harder to see.)

Color Key

☐ light colors

• medium colors

☒ dark colors

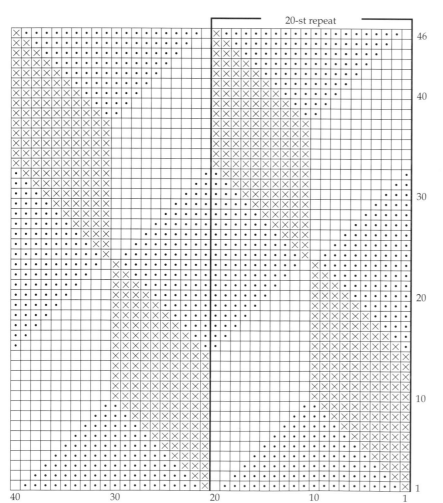

Now knit a sample swatch and try to recreate your impression of the color scheme in your chosen painting. The key word here is impression. This exercise isn't about trying to recreate the painting; it's about interpreting it in your own way, making a note of combinations that appeal to you, and putting together combinations that you might not have thought of previously.

As a first step, turn your reference postcard upside down. It sounds weird, but this makes it easier to concentrate on the colors. This is a tried-and-true technique in drawing and painting, and there's absolutely no reason you shouldn't apply it when designing in other mediums, too. It's a way of encouraging the right hemisphere of your brain (the visual side). If you look at the painting right side up, you'll probably be tempted to actually name the different elements (flower, horse, building, or whatever), which involves the left (verbal) side of the brain and distracts you from really looking at the colors involved.

Use stockinette stitch throughout, and work with manageable lengths of yarn (by that, I mean pieces no more than about one arm's length), joining in new colors wherever they seem appropriate. Think about the relative proportions of the colors. If your reference postcard shows, for example, a deep pink flower against a dark green leafy background, are both areas the same size—or is there far more green than pink? If it shows a golden-leafed tree in fall against a vibrant blue sky, do the leaves dominate, with only small patches of sky showing in between, or is the sky the main feature? Remember, however, you're not trying to recreate the painting in yarn, like a needlepoint picture. You're looking at the way the artist has used color and learning from it.

When I'm designing a garment for publication, I have to restrict the number of colors that I use. In this exercise, however, I want you to experiment with as much color as you like, trying different possibilities and working outside your natural comfort zone. It's a little scary at first, as you have to make your own decisions rather than relying on a pattern, but you'll soon discover how rich and expressive multi-shades can be. And when you happen across a combination that really sings out to you—a combination that makes your heart leap and brings a smile to your face—it's a truly magical moment!

Continue until you've knitted about an inch or so, continually referring to your reference painting. Do not bind off the piece, as you'll continue working on it in the next stage of the process.

At this point, I often find that people are worried that their knitting doesn't look neat and tidy. They've got lots of loose ends and are using yarns of different weights, so the tension is all over the place. Forget about all that! That isn't the point of the exercise at all. You're not supposed produce a perfect piece of knitting—and if you allow yourself to worry about it, you'll get so hung up on technique that you'll forget to analyze your color choices.

Above all, if you think you've made a "mistake" or don't like what you've done, do not, under any circumstances, pull it out and start over. If you find you've put together two colors that don't work, or the proportions of the colors are wrong, learn from it. You may even find that you can balance your "mistake" later in the piece by introducing the same color combination again.

By this stage, you'll have a piece of knitting that just looks like a randomly colored border to something else—but that's OK. You're not supposed to produce a finished piece. You may well be surprised at how mentally tiring it is—but you've started on the road to analyzing color combinations using your eyes, rather than your head.

Top: I start my color workshops with a huge pile of colored yarns in the middle of the floor, and as a demonstration, I usually make some appealing combinations and weed out discordant notes. I find myself putting a soft duck-egg blue with a group of pinks that starts to glow, or a burgundy red with a group of tobacco browns, or a soft lavender pink with grays or whites. These unexpected surprises are a real treat to discover.

Middle and bottom: These swatches of the Tumbling Blocks pattern show the different moods created by two different colorways.

Stage 2: Light, medium, and dark tones

The next stage in the process is to think about the tones, or values, of color. ("Tone" is simply a way of describing how light or dark a color is.) To do this, I give my students a knitting chart based on an old patchwork pattern known as Tumbling Blocks, which consists of three repeating diamond shapes—one light, one medium, and one dark. When the tonal values are assessed and placed correctly, the diamonds take on the appearance of interlocking boxes and the pattern looks three-dimensional.

Still referring to your reference postcard to keep track of the relative proportions of different colors in the piece, follow the chart, changing to a light-, medium-, or dark-toned yarn at the appropriate point. If your light tones are too dark, or your dark tones are too light, there won't be enough of a distinction between them and the mid-tones for the pattern to look three-dimensional. You won't always want the full range of light, medium, and dark tones in your work, but being able to recognize the relative values of colors is essential. With a strong, graphic pattern such as Tumbling Blocks, which has clearly defined blocks of color, it's easy to see whether or not you're assessing the tones correctly. Work at least one complete pattern of blocks, but do not bind off.

Tone is the aspect of working with color that most people find hardest to grasp. We tend to think of yellow, for example, as being a light color—but there are all kinds of yellows. A pale primrose yellow is light in tone, but a cadmium yellow or a deep canary yellow is more likely to be medium in tone. Greens can range from a very pale apple green to a viridian that's so dark it looks almost black. Conversely, two colors that you think of as being very different—let's say, green and pink—may actually be the same tone. Some people find that it helps to imagine the colors in front of them have been photocopied in black and white, so they become shades of gray.

To get used to assessing lots of different colors, try not to repeat the same colors in each diamond shape. If you use pale pinks and mauves in one light-toned diamond, for example, try knitting the next one using light blues or greens.

The other very important thing to bear in mind is that your perception of whether a color is light, medium, or dark in tone depends on its placement. To illustrate this, select a color that you think is medium in tone and place it first next to a very dark tone and then next to a very light tone. It will appear lighter when it's next to the dark tone and darker when it's next to the light one. Looking at a single color of yarn in isolation doesn't tell you anything: you have to look at colors in combination with each other.

You'll probably reach a point where you lose confidence in your abilities and feel you can no longer judge whether a color is light, medium, or dark. Almost everyone experiences this at some stage—but that's only because you're looking at colors in a new way and trying to assess how they relate to one another. I promise you, it will get easier.

Stage 3: Gradations of tone and color

What appears to be a solid block of color is rarely, if ever, completely solid. If someone asks you to describe a rose, for example, you might tell them that it's red—but that's only part of the story. A single bloom may contain shades ranging from deep crimson through scarlet to pinky-white, with almost imperceptible transitions from one shade to another. Solid blocks of color can look very dull and lifeless. These subtle distinctions and transitions are what bring your knitting to life and make it sparkle, like rays of sunlight dancing on water.

Now continue with the exercise from the previous stage, still following the Tumbling Blocks pattern—but this time, introduce other colors within each diamond shape, while still maintaining the light, medium, and dark values.

It's very hard to see your knitting clearly when it's bunched up on your lap, so every time you work a couple of rows in a new color, drape your knitting over the back of a chair or sofa so it hangs vertically. Stand across the room from it, and really look hard to see if your color choices are working. Better still, buy (or make) a corkboard to hang on the wall and pin your knitting to it so you can view it from a distance. You'll be amazed at how different it looks. Remember that a

Opposite: Students display their workshop samples with inspiration cards.

knitted design will always be seen from farther away than when it is in your lap. It's like the difference between standing so close to an oil painting in a gallery that you can see the individual brushstrokes, and then stepping back to view it as a whole.

Continue until you've completed at least the second repeat of the Tumbling Blocks pattern, then stand back and assess your progress. This is the point in my workshops at which all the swatches people have struggled to create are put on a board, creating a large, joyous tapestry of color. Knitters are often amazed that their humble efforts add up to such a glowing arrangement.

From inspiration to design

These are difficult concepts to grasp, and the only way to come to grips with them is to practice, practice, and then practice some more. Persevere and you will start to look at things differently. Instead of seeing a blue sea, you'll notice myriad shades of azure, turquoise, and aquamarine. Instead of seeing a field of green grass, you'll be able to

pick out numerous greens, yellows, and browns.

I've trained myself to look at things in this way, and now I do it instinctively. When I'm inspired to translate something into a knitwear design, I analyze the colors in the way I've described in my three-stage process: first, looking at the color combinations and the relative proportions of each color in the overall scheme; second, assessing the tonal range required; and third, putting in those subtle transitions from one shade to the next, to bring the color schemes to life.

The aim of this book is to share with you some of the things that inspire me as a designer. If you understand some of the design decisions I make, you will, I hope, be able to embark on a similar creative process for yourself. It's a very personal voyage of discovery. Every one of us is different; every one of us draws on his or her own interests and experiences. That's what makes the process of designing and creating things so infinitely fascinating.

Australia

I can remember digging deep holes in the sand as a boy at the Welsh seaside. As the holes got deeper, I thought I would soon reach Australia—the other side of the world from the UK, with its sun-kissed beaches, friendly people, and fascinating Aboriginal history.

When I finally did get there, years later, I had no idea how large the country really was. Flying across it to Sydney, I was amazed at the vastness below me. Endless desert plains were laid out, as flat as a massive stingray, interrupted only by the eruption of Uluru (Ayers Rock), an extraordinary copper pink mound settled into the scorched terra cotta earth. (This region is known as the Red Centre, part of the outback.) This was such a dramatic contrast from the baked desertscape we'd been passing over for hours.

Stepping out of my suburban motel room on the first morning of my trip, I saw a flock of shrieking, bright lime-green parrots dart across the early morning turquoise-blue sky. It all seemed so exotic, and a far cry from the blackbirds back in the UK. Flowers bloomed around well-maintained green lawns. Places in and near Sydney seemed strangely familiar, with English names like King's Cross, Euston, and Paddington, and neat terraced houses lining the streets. Overhanging verandas were decorated with ornate iron balustrades, mostly maintained with a smart coat of black gloss paint. Sydney's famous opera house resembled wind-filled sails, reflecting the country's love for the water. Around the famous Bondi Beach (where all the houses seemed to have views of this surfers' paradise), a string of beaches lined the coast under the carved-out cliff edges. These cliff walls were like folds of fabric, in shades of dusty pinks and soft putty-browns with cool gray tones—reminding me of Italian ice cream, in contrast to the rich reds of the desert soil. Keeping these shades in mind, I recreated them in an abstract vertical stripe, capturing the subtle tones of the cliffs and incorporating a shade of red from the color of the surrounding earth.

From left to right: Sunset at Uluru (Ayers Rock) in Australia; pastel tones in sandy cliffs; shadows caught in an early morning hot air balloon ride.

There are many color combinations you could apply to this pattern yourself—taking it into reds and purples with a shot of green, or replacing the red by going for a turquoise-blue. Another knit inspired by the colors from the outback is the Uluru Jacket, working with the lively greens of the foliage, soft orange of the earth, and the magenta shadows of the cactus flowers. This loose jacket is roomy and knitted in wools and cottons, making it quite cool, too!

Australia holds so many levels of inspiration. I took a hot air balloon ride near the Red Centre early one morning. Amazingly, the plant life on the desert floor resembles the Aboriginal paintings, soft dots of pale grasses on the deep desert floor. Probably the most powerful inspiration in Australia is the color that exists in the coral beds of the Great Barrier Reef—but that's a whole other story.

I visited Adelaide, Perth, Melbourne, Brisbane, Cairns, and Sydney, but Adelaide wins my vote for having the most charm and character. This old town is made up of small, handsome bungalows, with corrugated roofs and wrought-iron porches resembling oversized lacework. I was told at a museum that the first Irish settlers in Australia translated the family lace into braces of iron that became symbols of their identity. I only wish there was more individual detail of this kind used in today's architecture.

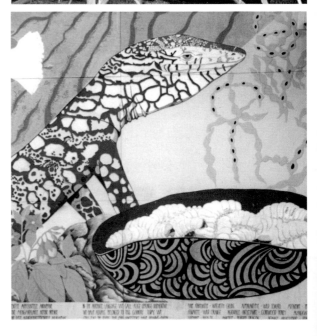

Most of Australia's population settled near the coastline. I did meet one gem of a lady attending our workshop who had traveled twenty-four hours by bus from a small farming town in the outback called Wagga Wagga. This is a very impoverished area where residents made blankets out of the old tailor's sample tweed books. These striking designs in men's suiting colors became known as "Wagga Waggas." I found one on display at the Powerhouse Museum in Sydney, and it inspired my first patchwork, which was featured in Rowan's *Patchwork & Quilting Book*. Patchwork is a new medium of expression for my color ideas.

Clockwise from bottom left: Exotic lizard pattern depicted in a street mural; tropical foliage; leopard-pattern hairstyle at a street market; burnt orange soil typical of the Australian outback.

Uluru Jacket

Materials

■ 2 1¾oz/50g balls (each approx 123yd/113m) of Rowan Yarns Wool Cotton (wool/cotton) each in #910 gypsy (A) and #946 elf (B)

■ 2 1¾oz/50g balls (each approx 142yd/130m) of RYC Classic Cashsoft DK (wool/microfiber/cashmere) in #511 madame (C)

■ 1 ball in #520 bloom (D)

■ 2 1¾oz/50g balls (each approx 124yd/113m) of Rowan Yarns Scottish Tweed DK (wool) in #19 peat (E)

■ 2 1¾oz/50g balls (each approx 191yd/175m) of Rowan Yarns 4 Ply Soft (wool) in #367 leafy (F)

■ 1 1¾oz/50g ball (approx 191yd/175m) of Rowan Yarns Felted Tweed (wool/alpaca/viscose) in #155 pickle (G)

■ 2 1¾oz/50g balls (each approx 131yd/120m) of Jaeger Yarns Matchmaker Merino DK (wool) each in #898 pumpkin (H), #656 cherry (I), and #894 geranium (J)

■ 1 ball in #655 burgundy (K)

■ One pair each sizes 4 and 6 (3.5 and 4mm) needles OR SIZE TO OBTAIN GAUGE

■ Two each sizes 4 and 6 (3.5 and 4mm) circular needles, 24"/60cm long

■ Bobbins

Sizes

One size fits most

Finished Measurements

■ Bust (closed) 72"/183cm

■ Length 26"/66cm

■ Upper arm 20"/51cm

Gauge

22 sts and 28 rows to 4"/10cm over St st and chart pat using larger needles.

TAKE TIME TO CHECK YOUR GAUGE.

Notes

1 Narrow horizontal stripes are worked with 2 strands held tog for a tweed effect.

2 Use 2 strands of F held tog throughout when working solid areas. When working narrow horizontal stripes, use 1 strand of F and 1 strand of contrasting color for the tweed effect.

3 Do not carry colors across; use a separate bobbin of color for each color section.

4 When changing colors, pick up new color from under dropped color to prevent holes.

5 Keep color changes on WS side of work.

BACK

With smaller circular needle and A, cast on 198 sts. Work back and forth using 2nd circular needle. Work in garter st for 4 rows. Change to larger circular needles. Cont in St st, work chart beg and end as indicated through row 180. Bind off all sts foll color pat.

LEFT FRONT

With smaller needles and A, cast on 99 sts. Work in garter st for 4 rows. Change to larger needles. Cont in St st, work chart beg and end as indicated through row 155.

Neck shaping

Row 156 (WS) Bind off 7 sts, work to end. Cont to bind off 3 sts from neck edge twice, then dec 1 st at neck edge every row 9 times—77 sts. Work even through row 180. Bind off all sts foll color pat.

RIGHT FRONT

With smaller needles and A, cast on 99 sts. Work in garter st for 4 rows. Change to larger needles. Cont in St st, work chart beg and end as indicated through row 154. Cont to shape neck as for left front, reversing all shaping.

SLEEVES

With smaller needles and A, cast on 54 sts. Work in rev St st for 4 rows, then in St st for 2 rows. Change to larger needles. Cont in St st and work chart, beg and end as indicated. AT THE SAME TIME, inc 1 st each side every 3rd row 28 times—110 sts. Work even through row 90. Bind off all sts foll color pat.

FINISHING

Block pieces to measurements. Sew shoulder seams.

Left front band

With RS facing, smaller needles and A, pick up and k 132 sts evenly spaced along left front edge. Work in garter st for 3 rows. Bind off all sts loosely knitwise.

Right front band

Work as for left front band.

Neckband

With RS facing, smaller needles and A, pick up and k 110 sts evenly spaced along neck edge. Work in garter st for 3 rows. Bind off all sts loosely knitwise. Place markers 10"/25.5cm down from shoulders on back and fronts. Sew sleeves to armholes between markers. Sew side and sleeve seams.

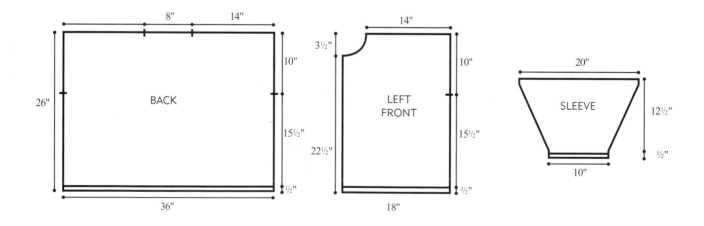

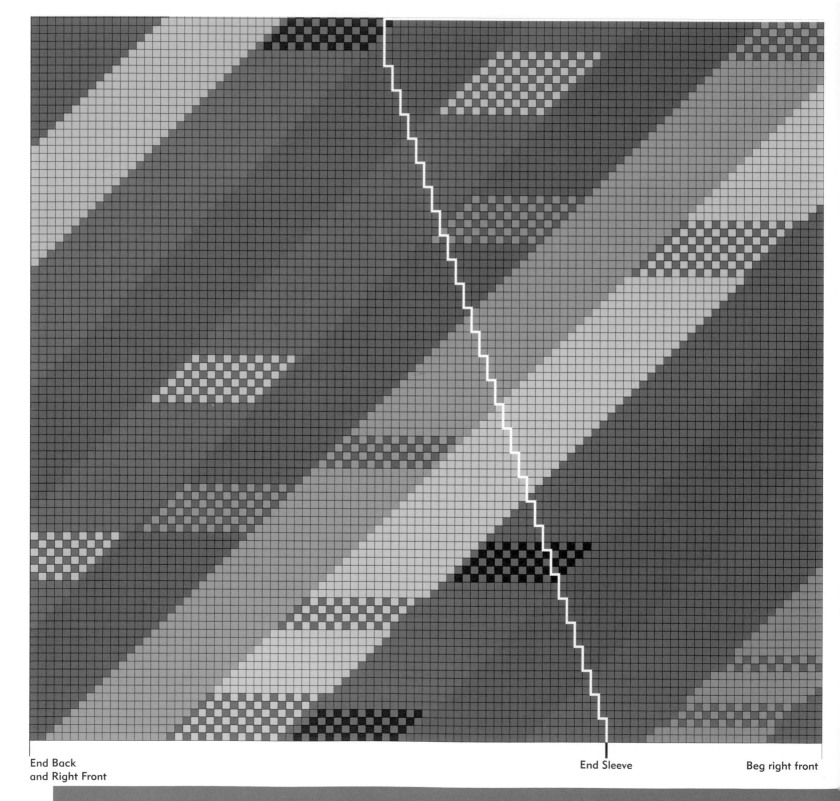

End Back
and Right Front

End Sleeve

Beg right front

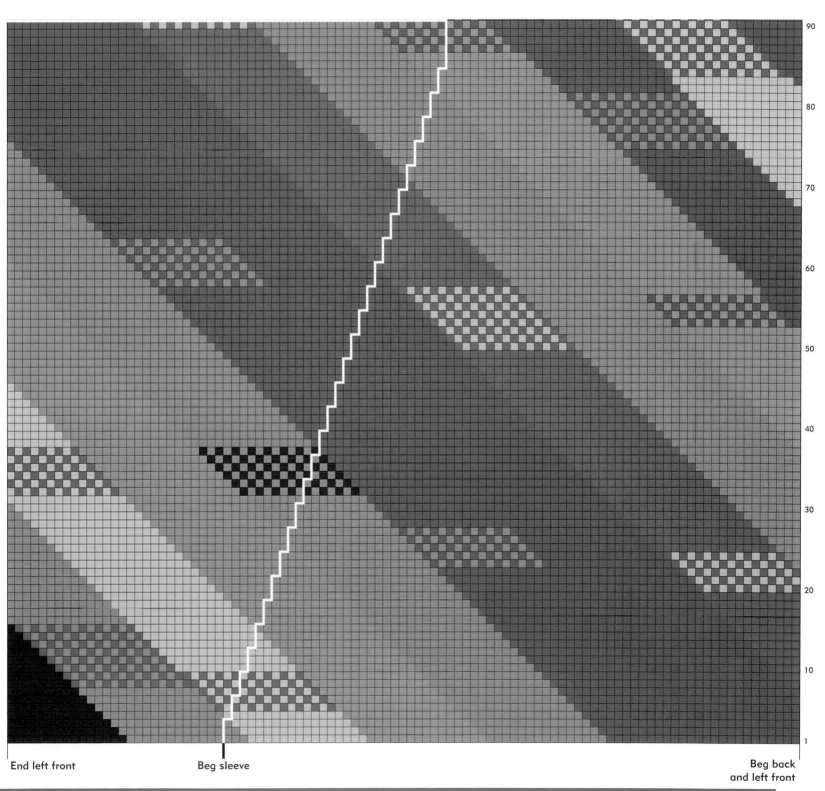

End left front

Beg sleeve

Beg back
and left front

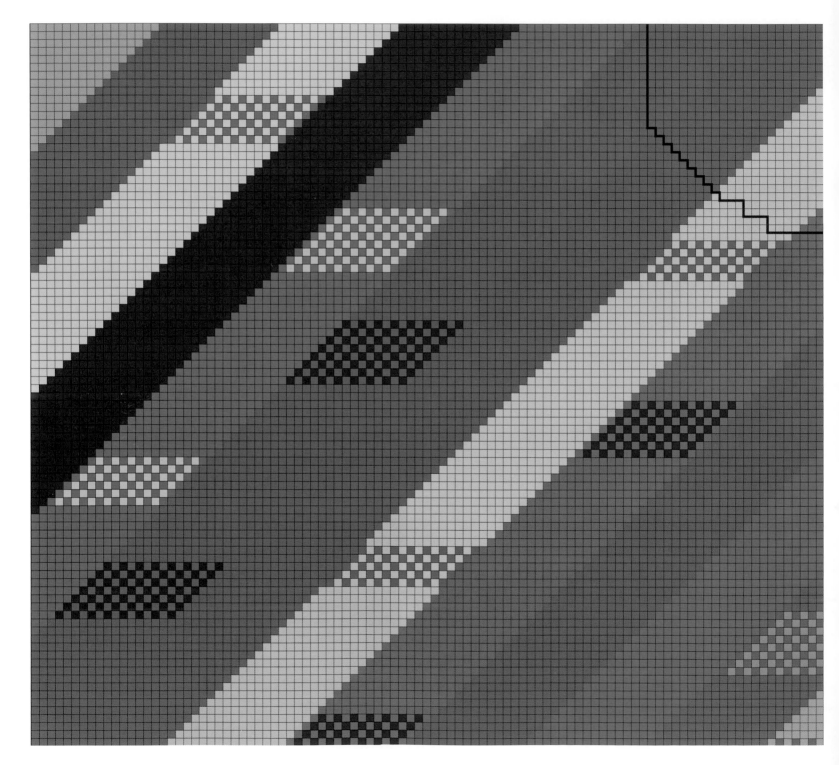

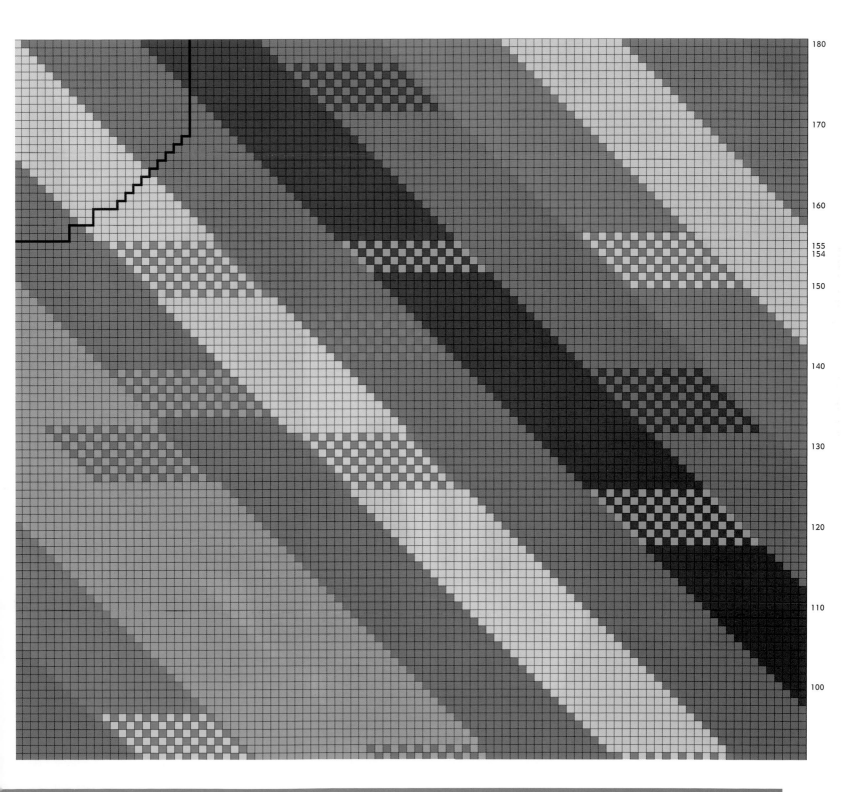

180
170
160
155
154
150
140
130
120
110
100

Swing Coat

Materials

- 2 (3) 1¾oz/50g balls (each approx 142yd/130m) of RYC Classic Cashcotton DK (cotton/polyamide/angora/viscose/cashmere) each in #606 quartz (A) and #604 geranium (B)

- 2 (3) 1¾oz/50g balls (each approx 142yd/130m) of RYC Classic Cashsoft DK (extra fine merino/microfiber/cashmere) each in #506 crush (C), #512 poppy (D) and #517 donkey (E)

- 2 (3) 1¾oz/50g balls (each approx 197yd/180m) of RYC Classic Cashcotton 4 Ply (cotton/polyamide/angora/viscose/cashmere) in #906 chintz (F)

- One pair each sizes 7 and 8 (4.5 and 5mm) needles OR SIZE TO OBTAIN GAUGE

- Two size 7 (4.5mm) circular needles, 24"/60cm long

- Bobbins

- Five ¾"/19mm buttons

Sizes

Instructions are written for size X-Small/Small. Changes for Medium/Large are in parentheses.

Finished Measurements

- Bust (closed) 41 (45)"/104 (114.5)cm

- Length 28 (28½)"/71 (72.5)cm

- Upper arm 20 (21)"/51 (53.5)cm

Gauge

16 sts and 24 rows to 4"/10cm over St st and chart pat using larger needles and 2 strands of A held tog.

TAKE TIME TO CHECK YOUR GAUGE.

Notes

1 Use 2 strands of A, B, C, D and E held tog throughout.

2 Use 3 strands of F held tog throughout.

3 Do not carry colors across; use a separate bobbin of color for each color section.

4 When changing colors, pick up new color from under dropped color to prevent holes.

5 Keep color changes on WS side of work.

STITCH GLOSSARY

Short row wrap and turn (w&t)

RS

1 Wyib, sl next st purlwise.

2 Move yarn between the needles to the front.

3 Sl the same st back to LH needle. Turn work, bring yarn to the WS between needles. One st is wrapped. When short rows are completed, work to just before wrapped st, insert RH needle under the wrap and knitwise into the wrapped st, k them tog.

WS

1 Wyif, sl next st purlwise.

2 Move yarn between the needles to the back of work.

3 Sl the same st back to LH needle. Turn work, bring yarn to the WS between the needles. One st is wrapped. When short rows are complet-ed, work to just before wrapped st, insert RH needle from behind into the back lp of the wrap and place on LH needle; p wrap tog with st on needle.

K2, P2 RIB

(multiple of 4 sts plus 2)

Row 1 (RS) K2, *p2, k2; rep from * to end.
Row 2 P2, *k2, p2; rep from * to end.
Rep rows 1 and 2 for k2, p2 rib.

BACK

With smaller needles and 2 strands of A held tog, cast on 122 (130) sts. Work in k2, p2 rib for 3 rows. Change to larger needles and F. Purl next row. Cont in St st and work chart, beg and end as indicated. Work through row 104, AT SAME TIME, dec 1 st each side every 5th row 20 times—82 (90) sts.

Armhole shaping

Bind off 3 (4) sts at beg of next 2 rows. Dec 1 st each side every row 3 times—70 (76) sts. Work even through row 164 (168). Bind off.

LEFT FRONT

With smaller needles and 2 strands of A held tog, cast on 62 (66) sts. Work in k2, p2 rib for 3 rows. Change to larger needles and F. Purl next row, dec 1 st—61 (65) sts. Cont in St st and work chart, beg and end as indicated. Work through row 104, AT SAME TIME, dec 1 st at side edge every 5th row 20 times—41 (45) sts.

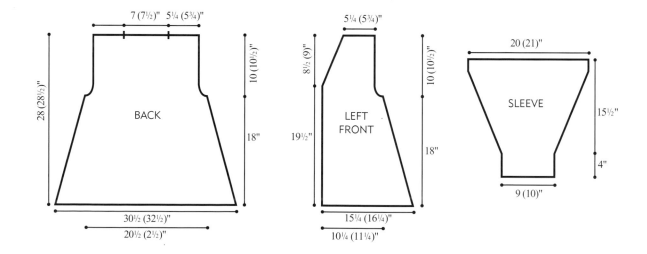

Armhole shaping

Row 105 (RS) Bind off 3 (4) sts, work to end. Purl next row. Dec 1 st at armhole edge on next row, then every row twice more—35 (38) sts. Work even through row 114.

Neck shaping

Dec 1 st at neck edge on next row, then every 3rd row 13 (14) times more—21 (23) sts. Work even through row 164 (168). Bind off.

RIGHT FRONT

With smaller needles and 2 strands of A held tog, cast on 62 (66) sts. Work in k2, p2 rib for 3 rows. Change to larger needles and F. Purl next row, dec 1 st—61 (65) sts. Cont in St st and work chart, beg and end as indicated. Work through row 105, AT SAME TIME, dec 1 st at side edge every 5th row 20 times—41 (45) sts.

Armhole shaping

Row 106 (WS) Bind off 3 (4) sts, work to end. Dec 1 st at armhole edge on next row, then every row twice more—35 (38) sts. Work even through row 114. Shape neck as for left front.

SLEEVES

With larger needles and 2 strands of A held tog, cast on 36 (40) sts. Cont in St st and work chart, beg and end as indicated. Work even through row 24. Inc 1 st each side on next row, then every 3rd row 8 times more, then every 4th row 13 times—80 (84) sts. Work even through row 116. Bind off.

FINISHING

Block pieces to measurements. Sew shoulder seams. On each front, place a yarn marker at beg of neck shaping. Place markers for 5 button-holes along right front edge, with the first 6"/15cm from lower edge, the last at beg of neck shaping and the others evenly spaced between.

Front bands and shawl collar

With RS facing, circular needle and 2 strands of A held tog, pick up and k 122 (125) sts along right front edge to shoulder, 34 (36) sts across back neck edge to shoulder, then 122 (125) sts along left front edge—278 (286) sts. Work back and forth using 2nd circular needle. Beg with row 2, work in k2, p2 rib for 1 row.

Buttonhole row (RS) *Work in rib to marker, yo, work 2 sts tog; rep from * 4 times more, rib to end.

Beg short row shaping

Short row 1 (WS) Work in rib to right front neck marker, w&t.

Short row 2 Work in rib to left front neck marker, w&t.

Short row 3 Work in rib to 2 sts before wrapped st, w&t. Rep row 3 until collar measures 5¾"/14.5cm from beg.

Next 2 rows Work to end, hiding wraps. Bind off all sts loosely in rib. Set in sleeves. Sew side and sleeve seams. Sew on buttons.

Color Key

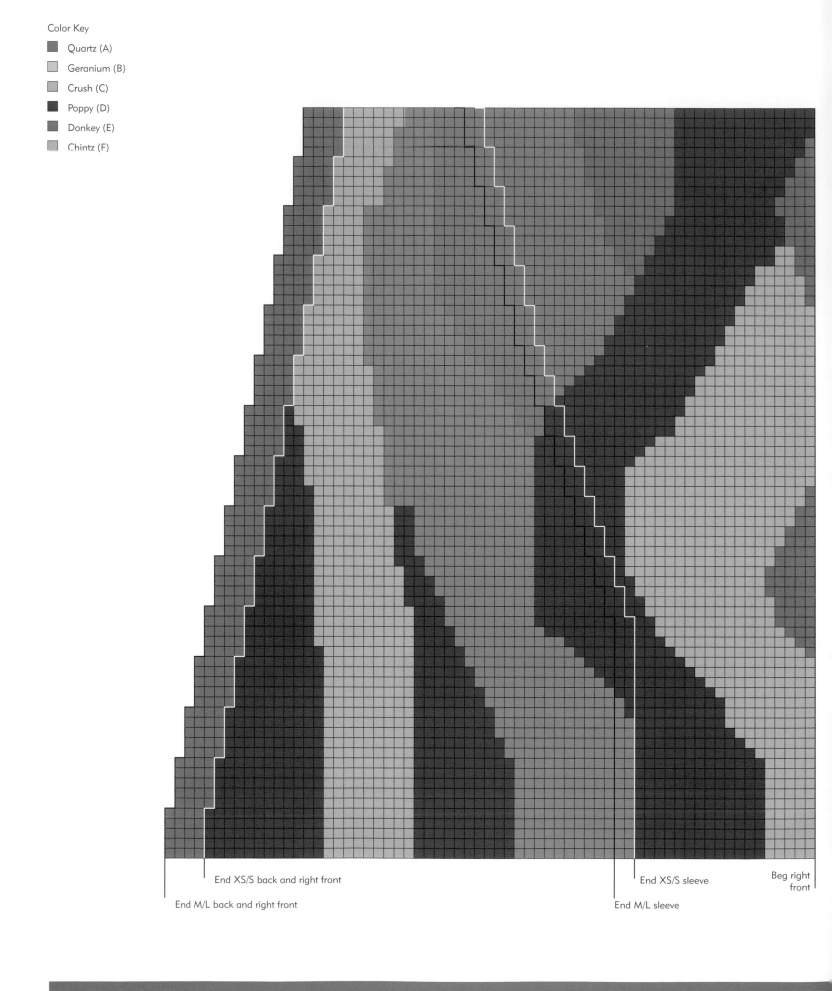

- ■ Quartz (A)
- ■ Geranium (B)
- ■ Crush (C)
- ■ Poppy (D)
- ■ Donkey (E)
- ■ Chintz (F)

End XS/S back and right front

End M/L back and right front

End XS/S sleeve

Beg right front

End M/L sleeve

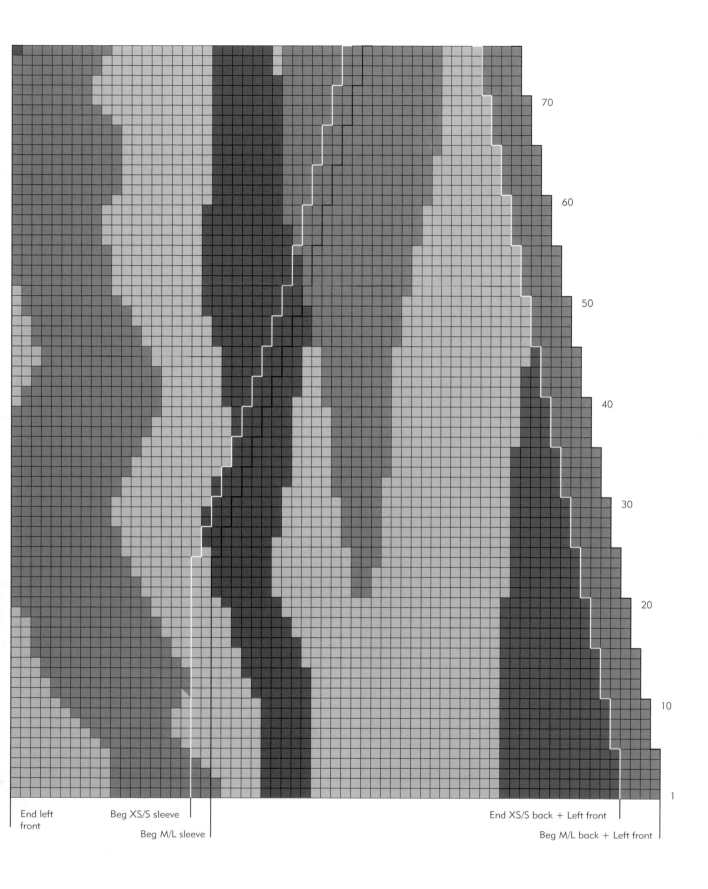

70

60

50

40

30

20

10

1

End left
front

Beg XS/S sleeve

Beg M/L sleeve

End XS/S back + Left front

Beg M/L back + Left front

Color Key

- ■ Quartz (A)
- ■ Geranium (B)
- ■ Crush (C)
- ■ Poppy (D)
- ■ Donkey (E)
- ■ Chintz (F)

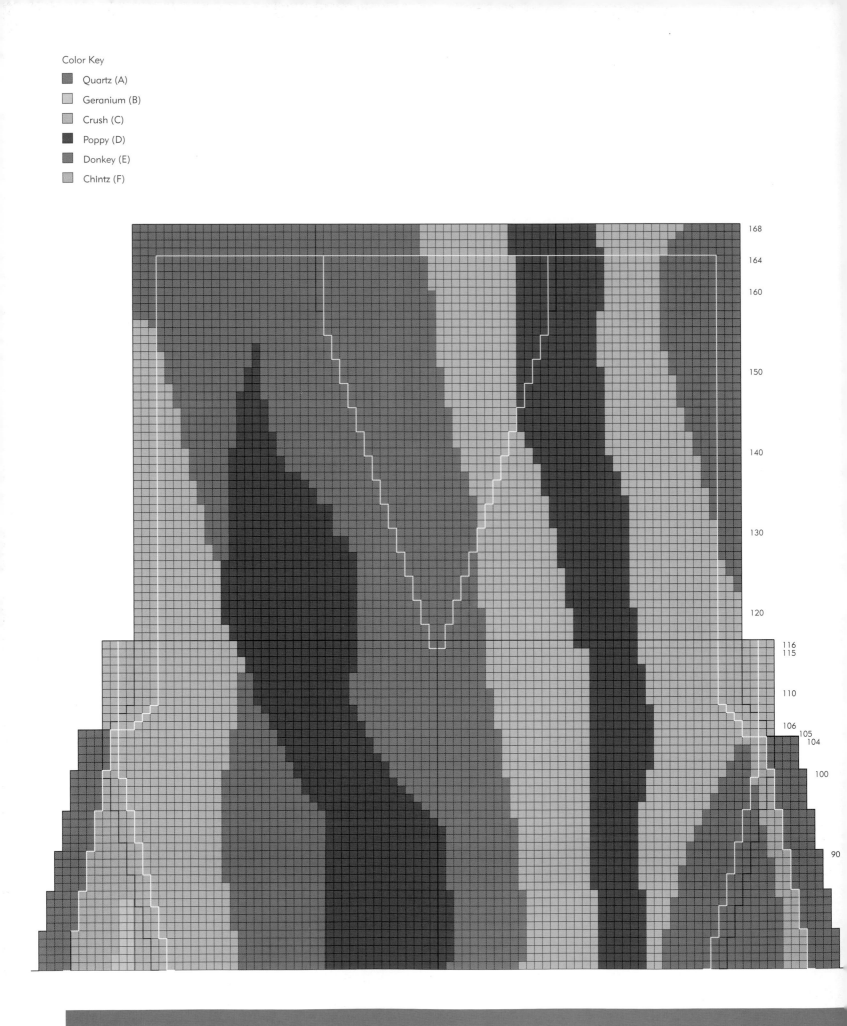

Great Britain

England has a reputation for gray, rainy days, but when I think about the British Isles, what strikes me are the incredibly lush, ever-changing fields and farms of the countryside.

The land is laced by a cobweb of narrow lanes banked by undulating hedgerows. The weathered stone walls, having stood the test of time, weave their way across verdant hillsides in the Cotswolds, Scotland, Yorkshire, Wales, and Ireland; their tonal palette and texture are among the defining elements of the British Isles.

AKaffe was asked in a recent lecture, "If you could only work with one color, what would it be?" His reply — "shades of gray" — amazed the audience, as he is so well-known for his flamboyant palette. There is something very satisfying, however, about working tone on tone. One advantage of Britain's gray weather is that it reveals a subtler palette, which would be washed out by glaring sunlight.

From left to right: Warm ocher tones in these cliffs offset the stoney grays; winter landscape of the English countryside; distressed texture on an English garden wall.

For Rowan's magazine collection, I have knitted several versions of a design called "Old Tiles"; here, I played with the same idea but used well over 100 different neutral shades in bouclé, silk, mohair, and wool for this highly detailed pillow design. There is something very satisfying in working with unlimited colors. I love using these multitones of gray, steely blue, warm pink, and brown. My only rule of thumb is to eliminate contrast and allow the tones to merge and smolder together, separated by charcoal-gray grouting. The piece is quite fine, done on a US 3 (3.25mm) needle, using mostly 4-ply or fingering-weight yarn.

On a playful note (and letting my cheeky side come out), I had to design something as an homage to our splendid British Royal Family, who keeps us all intrigued. I've also included a jacket with a dramatic stormy winter mood to it, reminding me of late afternoon and winter nights.

Above: Household nuts and bolts laid out in richly-colored boxes.

Old Tiles Pillow

Materials

- 4 .87oz/25g balls (each approx 120yd/110m) of Rowan Yarns Scottish Tweed 4 Ply (wool) in #20 mallard (A)

- 1 ball each in #14 heath (B), #8 herring (C), #4 storm grey (D), #1 grey mist (E) and #2 machair (F)

- 2 .87oz/25g balls (each approx 230yd/210m) of Rowan Yarns Kid Silk Haze (mohair/silk) each in #600 dewberry (G), #588 drab (H), and #589 majestic (I)

- One pair size 6 (4mm) needles OR SIZE TO OBTAIN GAUGE

- Bobbins

- Ten ¾"/19mm buttons

- Two 14" x 14"/38 x 38cm pillow forms

Finished Measurements

- 14" x 14"/35.5 x 35.5cm

Gauge

20 sts and 28 rows to 4"/10cm over St st and chart pat using size 6 (4mm) needles and 2 strands held tog.

TAKE TIME TO CHECK YOUR GAUGE.

Notes

1 Use 2 strands of yarn held tog throughout.

2 Do not carry colors across; use a separate bobbin of color for each color section.

3 When changing colors, pick up new color from under dropped color to prevent holes.

4 Keep color changes on WS side of work.

FRONT

With 2 strands of A held tog, cast on 80 sts. Knit next 6 rows.

Beg chart

Row 1 (RS) With A, k3, beg chart at st 1 and k to st 74, with A, k3.

Row 2 With A, k3, beg chart at st 74 and p to st 1, with A, k3. Cont to work as established to row 92, with 3 sts each side in garter st using A and rem sts in St st. With A only, knit next 6 rows. Bind off all sts knitwise.

BACK

Bottom half

With 2 strands of A held tog, cast on 80 sts. Knit next 6 rows.

Row 1 (RS) Knit.

Row 2 K3, p74, k3. Rep these 2 rows 39 times more. Knit next 8 rows for buttonband. Bind off all sts knitwise. Place markers for 5 buttons on buttonband, with the first and last 2½"/6.5cm from side edges and the others evenly spaced between.

Top half

Work as for bottom half, rep rows 1 and 2 43 times. Knit next 4 rows.

Buttonhole row (RS) *K to marker, yo, k2tog; rep from * 4 times more, k to end. Knit next 3 rows. Bind off all sts knitwise.

FINISHING

Block pieces to measurements. Lap back buttonhole band over button band; pin together along length of bands. With RS facing, sew front and back together around all edges. Remove pins. Turn RS out. Sew on buttons to correspond to buttonholes. Insert pillow form; button closed.

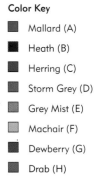

Color Key

- ▪ Mallard (A)
- ▪ Heath (B)
- ▪ Herring (C)
- ▪ Storm Grey (D)
- ▪ Grey Mist (E)
- ▪ Machair (F)
- ▪ Dewberry (G)
- ▪ Drab (H)
- ▪ Majestic (I)

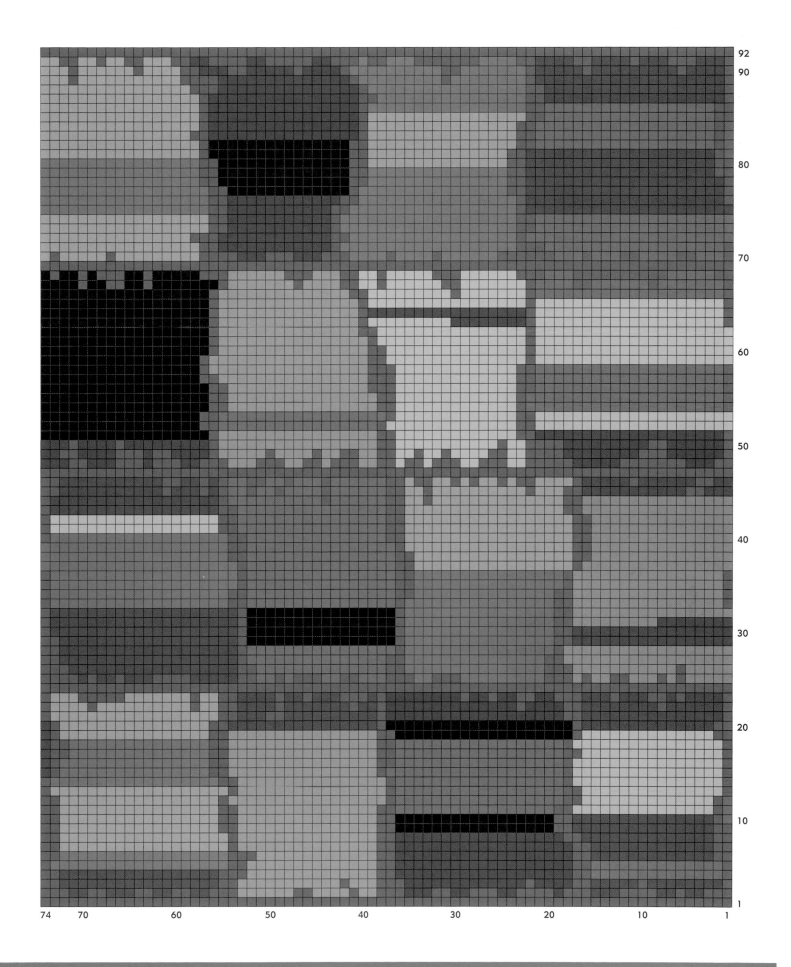

Crown Pillow

Materials

- 1 3½oz/100g ball (each approx 186yd/170m) of Rowan Yarns Scottish Tweed Aran (wool) in #9 rust (A)

- 1 ball each in #24 porridge (C) and #16 thistle (D)

- 1 .87oz/25g ball (each approx 120yd/110m) of Rowan Yarns Scottish Tweed 4 Ply (wool) in #11 sunset (B)

- 1 1¾oz/50g ball (each approx 124yd/113m) of Rowan Yarns Scottish Tweed DK (wool) in #11 sunset (B)

- 1 .87oz/25g ball (each approx 104yd/95m) of Rowan Yarns Lurex Shimmer (viscose/polyester) each in #330 copper (E), #332 antique white gold (F), #339 midnight (G), and #331 claret (H)

- One pair each sizes 7 and 8 (4.5 and 5mm) needles OR SIZE TO OBTAIN GAUGE

- Bobbins

- Five 1⅛"/28mm buttons

- 18" x 20"/45.5 x 51cm pillow form

Finished Measurements

- 18" x 20"/45.5 x 51cm

Gauge

17 sts and 24 rows to 4"/10cm over St st and chart pat using larger needles and A.

TAKE TIME TO CHECK YOUR GAUGE.

Notes

1 For colors A, C and D, use one strand of yarn throughout.

2 For color B, use 1 strand of Scottish Tweed 4 Ply #11 sunset and 1 strand of Scottish Tweed DK #11 sunset held tog throughout.

3 For colors E, F, G and H, use 2 strands of yarn held tog throughout.

4 Do not carry colors across; use a separate bobbin of color for each color section.

5 When changing colors, pick up new color from under dropped color to prevent holes.

6 Keep color changes on WS side of work.

STRIPE PATTERN

Working in St st, *work 11 rows A, 11 rows B; rep from * (22 rows) for stripe pat.

FRONT

With larger needles and A, cast on 84 sts. Cont in stripe pat for 22 rows.

Beg chart pat

Row 1 (RS) With A, k9, beg chart at st 1 and k to st 66, with A, k9.

Row 2 With A, p9, beg chart at st 66 and p to st 1, with A, p9. Cont to work as established to row 66. AT THE SAME TIME, cont to work in stripe pat. When chart is completed, work 11 rows A and 11 rows B. Bind off.

BACK

Bottom half

With larger needles and A, cast on 84 sts. Cont in stripe pat and work until 44 rows have been completed. Change to A and work for 10 rows. Change to smaller needles and cont as folls:

Button band

Work in k1, p1 rib for 5 rows. Bind off all sts loosely in rib. Place markers for 5 buttons on button band, with the first and last 2½"/6.5cm from side edges and the others evenly spaced between.

Top half

With larger needles and B, cast on 84 sts. Cont in stripe pat and work until 55 rows have been completed, end with a RS row. Change to smaller needles and cont with B only as folls:

Buttonhole band

Work in k1, p1 rib for 1 row.

Buttonhole row (RS) *Work in rib to marker, yo, k2tog; rep from * 4 times more, work in rib to end. Cont in rib for 3 more rows. Bind off all sts loosely in rib.

FINISHING

Block pieces to measurements. Lap back buttonhole band over button band; pin together along length of bands. With RS facing, sew front and back together around all edges. Remove pins. Turn RS out. Sew on buttons to correspond to buttonholes. Insert pillow form; button closed.

Color Key

■ Rust (A)

■ Sunset (B)

□ Porridge (C)

■ Thistle (D)

■ Copper (E)

■ Antique White Gold (F)

■ Midnight (G)

■ Claret (H)

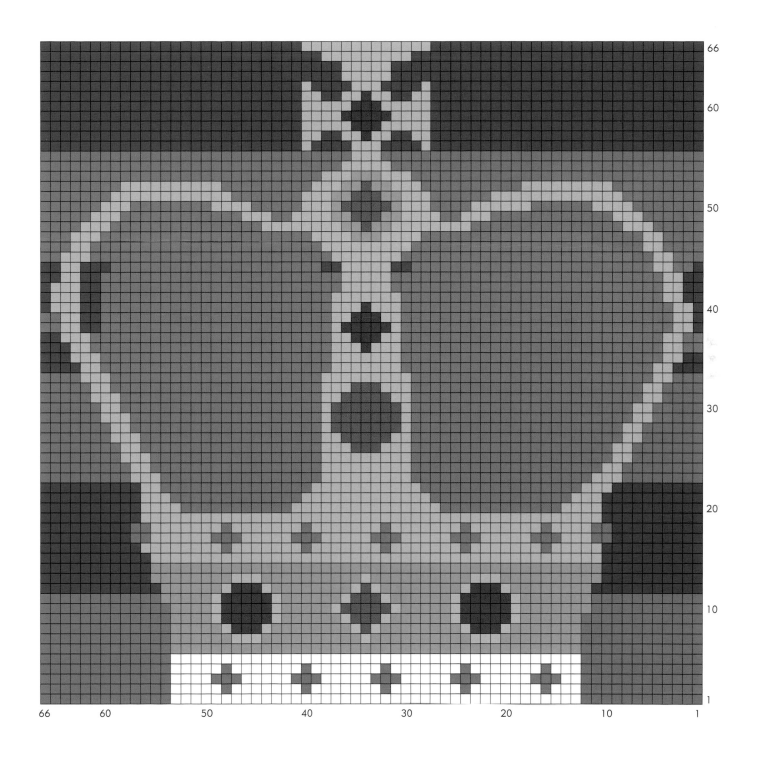

Crown Sweater

Materials

- 5 (5, 6) 3½oz/100g balls (each approx 186yd/170m) of Rowan Yarns Scottish Tweed Aran (wool) in #9 rust (A)

- 1 ball each in #24 porridge (C) and #13 claret dark (D)

- 6 (6, 7) .87oz/25g balls (each approx 120yd/110m) of Rowan Yarns Scottish Tweed 4 Ply (wool) in #11 sunset (B)

- 6 (6, 7) 1¾oz/50g balls (each approx 124yd/113m) of Rowan Yarns Scottish Tweed DK (wool) in #11 sunset (B)

- 1.87oz/25g balls (each approx 104yd/95m) of Rowan Yarns Lurex Shimmer (viscose/polyester) each in #330 copper (E), #332 antique white gold (F), #339 midnight (G), and #331 claret (H)

- One pair each sizes 7 and 8 (4.5 and 5mm) needles OR SIZE TO OBTAIN GAUGE

- Stitch holders

- Bobbins

Sizes

Instructions are written for Men's size Small. Changes for Medium and Large are in parentheses.

Finished Measurements

- Chest 44 (47, 51)"/111.5 (119.5, 129.5)cm

- Length 25 (25½, 26)"/63.5 (64.5, 66)cm

- Upper arm 18 (19, 20)"/45.5 (48, 51)cm

Gauge

17 sts and 24 rows to 4"/10cm over St st and chart pat using larger needles and A.

TAKE TIME TO CHECK YOUR GAUGE.

Notes

1 For colors A, C and D, use one strand of yarn throughout.

2 For color B, use 1 strand of Scottish Tweed 4 Ply #11 sunset and 1 strand of Scottish Tweed DK #11 sunset held tog throughout.

3 For colors E, F, G and H, use 2 strands of yarn held tog throughout.

4 Do not carry colors across; use a separate bobbin of color for each color section.

5 When changing colors, pick up new color from under dropped color to prevent holes.

6 Keep color changes on WS side of work.

K2, P2 RIB

(multiple of 4 sts plus 2)

Row 1 (RS) K2, *p2, k2; rep from * to end.

Row 2 P2, *k2, p2; rep from * to end.

Rep rows 1 and 2 for k2, p2 rib.

STRIPE PATTERN

Working in St st, *work 12 rows B, 12 rows A; rep from * (24 rows) for stripe pat.

BACK

With smaller needles and A, cast on 94 (98, 106) sts. Work in k2, p2 rib for 2"/5cm, inc 0 (2, 2) sts evenly spaced across last row and end with a WS row—94 (100, 108) sts. Change to larger needles and cont in stripe pat until piece measures 24 (24½, 25)"/61 (62, 63.5)cm from beg, end with a WS row.

Neck shaping

Next row (RS) K 34 (36, 39) sts, place center 26 (28, 30) sts on holder for back neck, join another ball of yarn, work to end. Working both sides at once, dec 1 st from each neck edge every row twice. Work even on 32 (34, 37) sts each side until piece measures 25 (25½, 26)"/63.5 (64.5, 66)cm from beg, end with a WS row. Bind off each side.

FRONT

Work ribbing as for back—94 (100, 108) sts. Change to larger needles and cont in stripe pat until 36 rows have been completed.

Beg chart pat

Row 1 (RS) With A, k 14 (17, 21) sts, beg chart at st 1 and k to st 66, with A, k 14 (17, 21) sts.

Row 2 With A, p 14 (17, 21) sts, beg chart at st 66 and p to st 1, with A, p 14 (17, 21) sts. Cont to work as established to row 66. AT THE SAME TIME, cont to work in stripe pat. When chart is completed, work even in stripe pat until piece measures 22 (22½, 23)"/56 (57, 58.5)cm from beg, end with a WS row.

Neck shaping

Next row (RS) K 44 (46, 49), place center 6 (8, 10) sts on holder for

front neck, join another ball of yarn, work to end. Working both sides at once, dec 1 st from each neck edge every row 12 times. Work even on 32 (34, 37) sts each side until piece measures same length as back to shoulder, end with a WS row. Bind off each side.

SLEEVES

With smaller needles and A, cast on 42 (42, 46) sts. Work in k2, p2 rib for 2"/5cm, end with a WS row. Change to larger needles. Cont in stripe pat and inc 1 st each side every 4th row 5 (10, 10) times, every 6th row 13 (10, 10) times—78 (82, 86) sts. Work even until piece measures 19 (19½, 20)"/48 (49.5, 51)cm from beg, end with a WS row. Bind off.

FINISHING

Block pieces to measurements. Sew right shoulder seam.

Neckband

With RS facing, smaller needles and A, pick up and k 78 (82, 86) sts evenly spaced along neck edge (including sts on holders). Beg with row 2, work in k2, p2 rib for 5 rows. Change to D. Bind off all sts loosely in rib. Sew left shoulder and neckband seam. Place markers 9 (9½, 10)"/23 (24, 25.5)cm down from shoulders on back and front. Sew sleeves to armholes between markers. Sew side and sleeve seams.

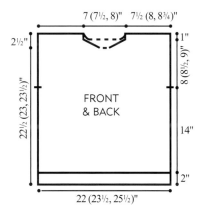

Color Key
- Rust (A)
- Sunset (B)
- Porridge (C)
- Claret Dark (D)
- Copper (E)
- Antique White Gold (F)
- Midnight (G)
- Claret (H)

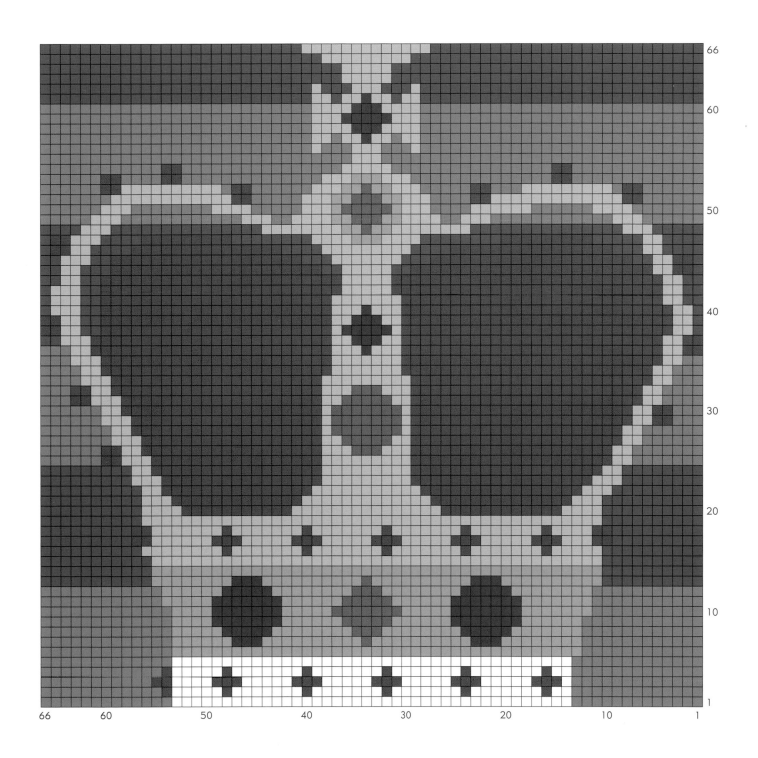

Landscape Jacket

Materials

- 3 (4, 4, 4) 1¾oz/100g balls (each approx 109yd/100m) of Rowan Yarns Yorkshire Tweed Chunky (wool) in #555 coast (A)

- 2 balls each in #550 damp (E), #553 pecan (F) and #551 string (H)

- 3 3½oz/100g balls (each approx 175yd/160m) of Rowan Yarns Yorkshire Tweed Aran (wool) each in #415 maze (B) and #413 muffin (D)

- 3 1¾oz/50g balls (each approx 123yd/113m) of Rowan Yarns Yorkshire Tweed DK (wool) in #348 lime leaf (C)

- 2 balls in #343 cheer (G)

- One pair each sizes 10½ and 11 (6.5 and 8mm) needles OR SIZE TO OBTAIN GAUGE

- Bobbins

- Stitch holder

- Five 1⅛"/28mm buttons

Sizes

Instructions are written for size Small. Changes for Medium, Large and X-Large are in parentheses.

Finished Measurements

- Chest (closed) 45 (48, 51, 54)"/114.5 (122, 129.5, 137)cm

- Length 31 (31½, 32, 32½)"/78.5 (80, 81, 82.5)cm

- Upper arm 13½ (14½, 15, 16½)"/34 (37, 38, 42)cm

Gauge

12 sts and 16 rows to 4"/10cm over St st and chart pat using larger needles and A.

TAKE TIME TO CHECK YOUR GAUGE.

Notes

1 Use 1 strand of Yorkshire Tweed Chunky (colors A, E, F and H) throughout.

2 Use 2 strands of Yorkshire Tweed Aran (colors B and D) or Yorkshire Tweed DK (colors C and G) held together throughout.

3 Do not carry colors across; use a separate bobbin of color for each color section.

4 When changing colors, pick up new color from under dropped color to prevent holes.

5 Keep color changes on WS side of work.

BACK

With smaller needles and A, cast on 67 (73, 77, 81) sts. Work in St st for 9 rows. Knit next row for turning ridge. Change to larger needles. Cont in St st and work chart I, beg and end as indicated. Work through row 14. Dec 1 st each side on next row, then every 12th row twice more—61 (67, 71, 75) sts. Work even through row 56. Inc 1 st each side on next row, then every 8th row twice more—67 (73, 77, 81) sts. Work through row 86.

Armhole shaping

Bind off 4 (5, 6, 6) sts at beg of next 2 rows, 2 sts at beg of next 2 rows, then dec 1 st each side every other row 5 (6, 6, 7) times—45 (47, 49, 51) sts. Work through row 120 (122, 124, 126).

Shoulder shaping

Using D (D, C, E) only, bind off 7 (7, 7, 8) sts at beg of next 2 rows, then 7 (8, 8, 8) sts at beg of next 2 rows. Bind off rem 17 (17, 19, 19) sts for back neck.

LEFT FRONT

With smaller needles and A, cast on 35 (38, 40, 42) sts. Work in St st for 9 rows. Knit next row for turning ridge. Change to larger needles. Cont in St st and work chart I, beg and end as indicated. Work through row 14. Dec 1 st at beg of next row, then at same edge every 12th row twice more—32 (35, 37, 39) sts. Work even through row 56. Inc 1 st at same edge on next row, then every 8th row twice more—35 (38, 40, 42) sts. Work through row 86.

Armhole shaping

Row 87 (RS) Bind off 4 (5, 6, 6) sts, work to end. Cont to shape armhole as foll: bind off 2 sts at armhole edge once, then dec 1 st every other row 5 (6, 6, 7) times—24 (25, 26, 27) sts. Work through row 107 (109, 111, 113).

Neck shaping

Row 108 (110, 112, 114) (WS) Bind off 5 (5, 6, 6) sts, work to end. Dec 1 st from neck edge on next row, then every row 4 times more—14 (15, 15, 16) sts. Work through row 120 (122, 124, 126).

Shoulder shaping

Using D (D, C, E) only, bind off 7 (7, 7, 8) sts at armhole edge once, then 7 (8, 8, 8) sts once. Place markers for 5 buttons along left front edge, with the first 8½"/21.5cm from turning ridge, the last ¾"/2cm from neck edge and the others evenly spaced between.

RIGHT FRONT

Work as for left front through row 87, reversing shaping. AT THE SAME TIME, work buttonholes opposite markers on left front as foll:
Buttonhole row (RS) K 2, yo, k2tog, work to end.

Armhole shaping

Row 88 (WS) Bind off 4 (5, 6, 6) sts, work to end. Cont to shape armhole as for left front—24 (25, 26, 27) sts. Work through row 108 (110, 112, 114).

Neck shaping

Row 109 (111, 113, 115) (RS) Bind off 5 (5, 6, 6) sts, work to end. Cont to shape neck and shoulder as for left front, reversing all shaping.

SLEEVES

With smaller needles and A, cast on 31 (33, 33, 35) sts. Work in St st for 9 rows. Knit next row for turning ridge. Change to larger needles. Cont in St st and work chart II, beg and end as indicated. Work through row 8 (8, 6, 4). Inc 1 st each on next row, then every 14th (14th, 12th, 10th) row 4 (4, 5, 6) times more—41 (43, 45, 49) sts. Work even through row 72.

Cap shaping

Bind off 4 (4, 4, 5) sts at beg of next 2 rows. Dec 1 st each side on next row, then every other row 7 (8, 9, 10) times more, then bind off 3 sts at beg of next 2 rows. Bind off rem 11 sts on row 92 (94, 96, 98).

FINISHING

Block pieces to measurements. Sew shoulder seams.

Left front edging

With RS facing, smaller needles and A, pick up and k 81 (83, 84, 86) sts evenly spaced along left front edge from neck edge to turning ridge. Work in garter st for 2 rows. Bind off all sts loosely knitwise.

Right front edging

With RS facing, smaller needles and A, pick up and k 81 (83, 84, 86) sts evenly spaced along right front edge from turning ridge to neck edge. Work in garter st for 2 rows. Bind off all sts loosely knitwise.

Collar

With RS facing, smaller needles and A, pick up and k 65 (65, 69, 69) sts evenly spaced along entire neck edge. Work in garter st for 4½ (4½, 5, 5)"/11.5 (11.5, 12.5, 12.5)cm. Bind off all sts loosely knitwise. Set in sleeves. Sew side and sleeve seams. Turn each band to WS along turning ridge and hem in place. Sew on buttons.

Color Key

- Coast (A)
- Maze (B)
- Lime Leaf (C)
- Muffin (D)
- Damp (E)
- Pecan (F)
- Cheer (G)
- String (H)

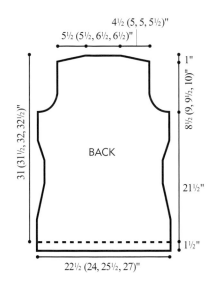

BACK

4½ (5, 5, 5½)"
5½ (5½, 6½, 6½)"
1"
8½ (9, 9½, 10)"
31 (31½, 32, 32½)"
21½"
1½"
22½ (24, 25½, 27)"

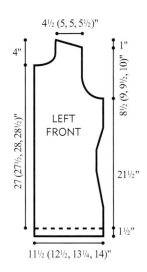

LEFT FRONT

4½ (5, 5, 5½)"
4"
1"
8½ (9, 9½, 10)"
27 (27½, 28, 28½)"
21½"
1½"
11½ (12½, 13¼, 14)"

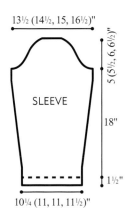

SLEEVE

13½ (14½, 15, 16½)"
5 (5½, 6, 6½)"
18"
1½"
10¼ (11, 11, 11½)"

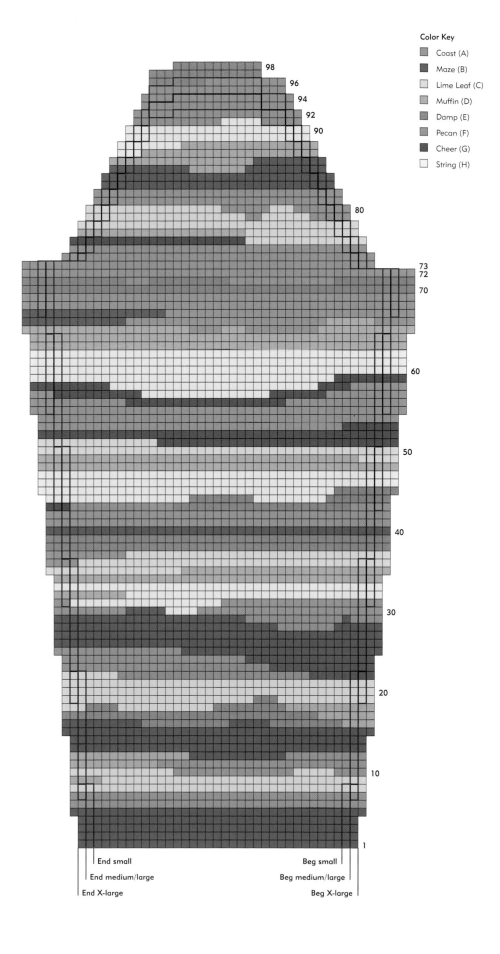

End small
End medium/large
End X-large

Beg small
Beg medium/large
Beg X-large

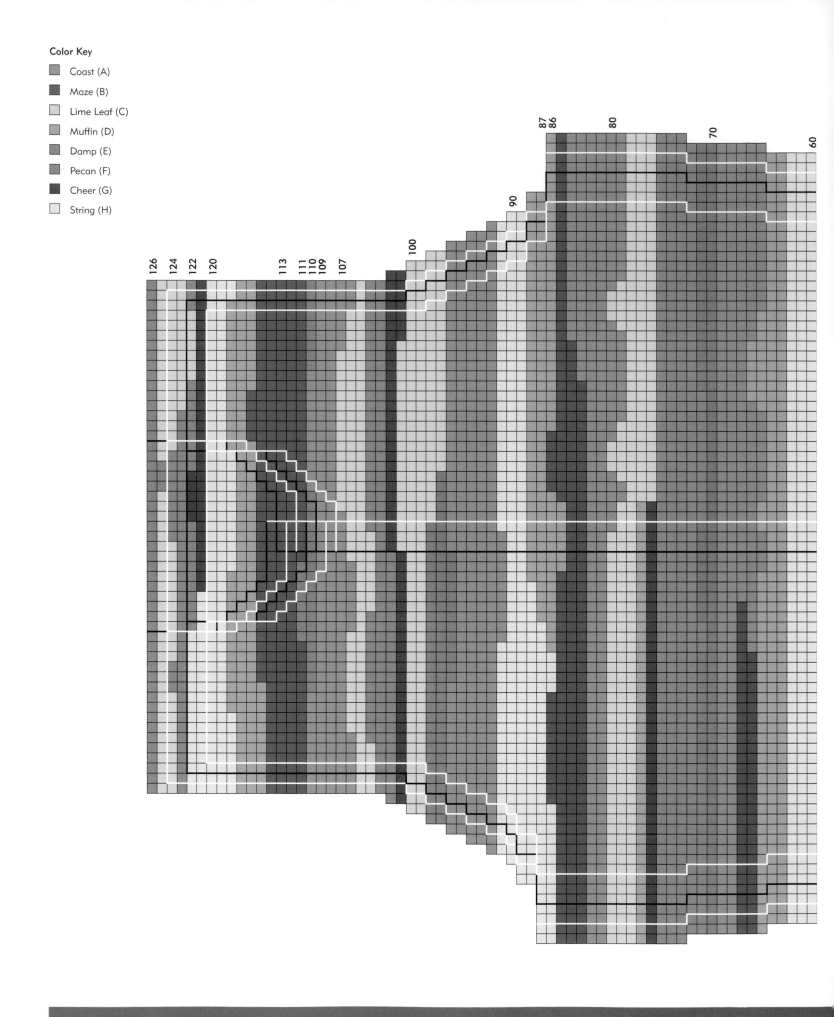

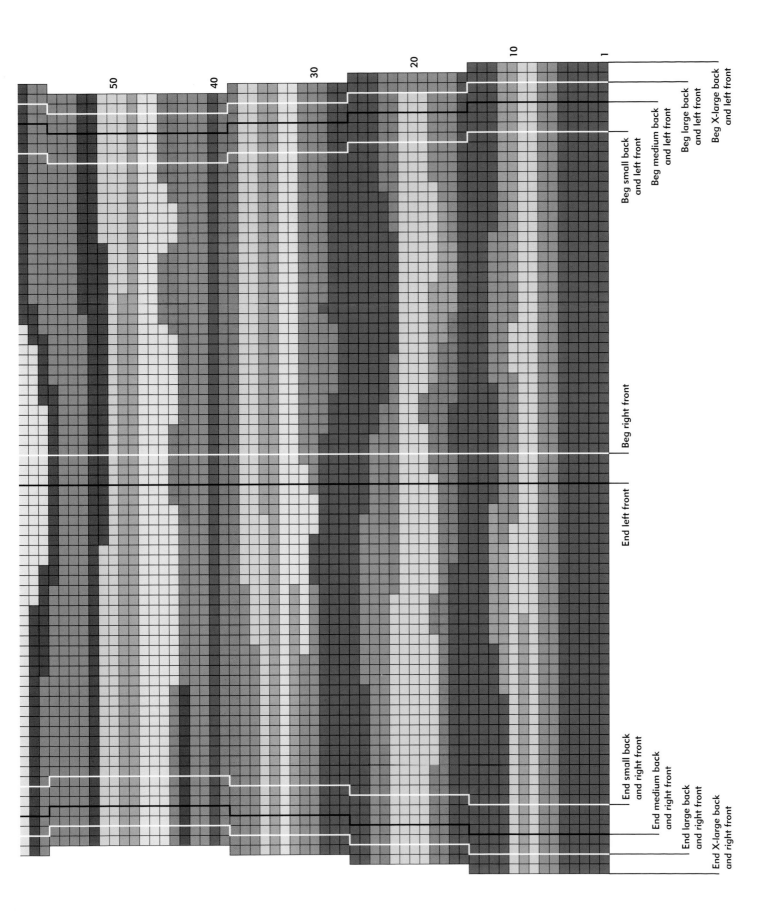

50 40 30 20 10 1

Beg small back
and left front

Beg medium back
and left front

Beg large back
and left front

Beg X-large back
and left front

Beg right front

End left front

End small back
and right front

End medium back
and right front

End large back
and right front

End X-large back
and right front

Guatemala

When the international charity Oxfam invited Kaffe and me to Guatemala to work with local craftspeople in creating some exciting new designs, we jumped at the chance.

I was overwhelmed by what I saw in Guatemala. It is the most colorful country I've ever come across, bar none. Color just seeps out of the ground. The clothes are inventive and fanciful. Both the men and women casually wear charming birds and flowers embroidered on and woven into their lavishly patterned clothing. The streets are filled with women wearing vibrantly colorful blouses that set off their black hair and tanned complexion. Occasionally you see a woman on her way to the market with a boldly striped blanket tied around her shoulder, the head of a child or the brilliant

plume of a rooster peeking out. The buildings, too, show this love of color: dusty pinks, soft turquoises, pale yellows, deep ochers, and golds don their walls.

We stayed in a beautiful small town called Lake Atitlán where makeshift stalls line the winding road to the lake edge. Boldly painted wooden fishing boats ferry passengers across the lake to a village at the foot of an impressive volcano. Besides the charm of the bustling food market, the most endearing quality is the embroidery on the knee-length trousers worn by the men of this village. The trousers are made of a pale blue striped fabric, whose surface dances with bright little embroidered birds. They wear them with a striped sash at the

Left to right: Women in the market; peppers resting in a beautiful striped blanket; villager collecting water.

waist, a gleaming white shirt, and an oversized
straw hat with a black band that matches their
moustaches—a dandy uniform, indeed.
Fortunately, I was able to purchase a pair of these
whimsical trousers. Each embroidered bird is
very colorful—just the inspiration for a children's
knit design.

Moving on from Lake Atitlán, our next port of call
was Chichicastenango. (The name makes me smile,
sounding as it does like rattling maracas—chi-chi-
castas!) This region is famous for its use of rose
motifs woven into the huipils (elaborate poncho-
style garments) worn by the women. The best
examples of these textiles are found at the weekly
market in the town's central square, below the
steps of the cathedral. A maze of narrow alleyways,
roofed over with plastic sheeting in shades of blue,
is home to stalls proudly selling fresh vegetables
and fruits to the locals, and textiles to the busloads
of tourists.

The frenzy of this bustling market stands in stark
contrast to the imposing dark cathedral entrance
where worshippers work their way up the steps
between the shoeshine boys and the vagabonds.
They carry calla lilies while chanting prayers. I felt
transported to a biblical scene in a medieval painting. Inside the vast church, the life-size religious
figures are lovingly draped in Hermès scarves and
other patterned fabrics.

I hope that you will be inspired to try knitting my interpretation of these sumptuous, overblown blossoms. If the background is a little strong for you, try a deep turquoise-blue. (Even a charcoal-gray would be handsome.) I leave it up to you to play with the idea.

Clockwise from bottom left: A beautifully subtle doorway; hand-embroidered jeans in luminous colors; two shots of a façade of a village church.

Flower Vest

Materials

■ 8 (9) 1¾oz/50g balls (each approx 126yd/115m) of Rowan Yarns Cotton Glace (cotton) in #815 excite (MC)

■ 1 ball each in #820 pick & mix (A), #812 ivy (B), #747 candy floss pink (C), #739 dijon (D), #741 poppy (E), #730 oyster (F), #817 maritime (G), #809 pier (H), #819 in the pink (I), and #811 tickle (J)

■ One pair each sizes 4 and 6 (3.5 and 4mm) needles OR SIZE TO OBTAIN GAUGE

■ Bobbins

Sizes

Instructions are written for size Small/Medium. Changes for Large/X-Large are in parentheses.

Finished Measurements

■ Bust 43 (47)"/109 (119.5)cm

■ Length 26½ (27)"/67.5 (68.5)cm

Gauge

23 sts and 32 rows to 4"/10cm over St st and chart pat using larger needles.

TAKE TIME TO CHECK YOUR GAUGE.

Notes

1 When changing colors, pick up new color from under dropped color to prevent holes.

2 Do not carry colors across. Use a separate bobbin of color for each color section.

3 Keep color changes on WS side of work.

BACK

With smaller needles and MC, cast on 124 (136) sts. Work in garter st for 6 rows. Change to larger needles. Cont in St st and work chart pat, beg and end as indicated. Work even through row 144, end with a WS row.

Armhole shaping

Bind off 8 (10) sts at beg of next 2 rows, then 4 sts at beg of next 4 rows. Dec 1 st each side every other row 9 times, every 4th row 3 times—68 (76) sts. Work even through row 208 (212). Bind off.

LEFT FRONT

With smaller needles and MC, cast on 62 (68) sts. Work in garter st for 6 rows. Change to larger needles. Cont in St st and work chart pat, beg and end as indicated. Work even through row 144, end with a WS row. Shape armhole at side edge as for back—34 (38) sts. Work even through row 189 (193), end with a RS row.

Neck shaping

Row 190 (194) (WS) Bind off 6 (7) sts, work to end. Dec 1 st at neck edge every row 10 times—18 (21) sts. Work even through row 208 (212). Bind off.

RIGHT FRONT

With smaller needles and MC, cast on 62 (68) sts. Work in garter st for 6 rows. Change to larger needles. Cont in St st and work chart pat, beg and end as indicated. Work even through row 145, end with a RS row. Shape armhole at side edge as for back—34 (38) sts. Work even through row 190 (194), end with a WS row. Cont to shape neck as for left front, reversing all shaping.

FINISHING

Block pieces to measurements. Sew shoulder seams.

Left front band

With RS facing, smaller needles and MC, pick up and k 136 (140) sts evenly spaced along left front edge. Beg with a p row, cont in St st and stripe pat as folls: 1 row B, 3 rows MC, 1 row E, 1 row MC. With MC only, k next row for turning ridge. Cont in St st for 5 rows. Bind off all sts loosely.

Right front band

Work as for left front band. Fold each front band to WS along turning ridge and hem in place.

Neckband

With RS facing, smaller needles and MC, pick up and k 88 (92) sts evenly spaced along entire neck edge. Cont to work as for left front band.

Armbands

With RS facing, smaller needles and MC, pick up and k 134 (146) sts evenly spaced along armhole edge. Beg with a p row, cont in St st and stripe pat as folls: 1 row MC, 1 row B, 1 row MC, 1 row E, 1 row MC. With MC only, p next row for turning ridge. Beg with a p row, cont in St st for 4 rows. Bind off all sts loosely. Sew side and armband seams. Fold each band to WS along turning ridge and hem in place.

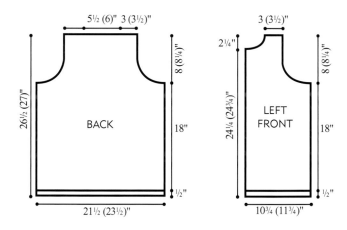

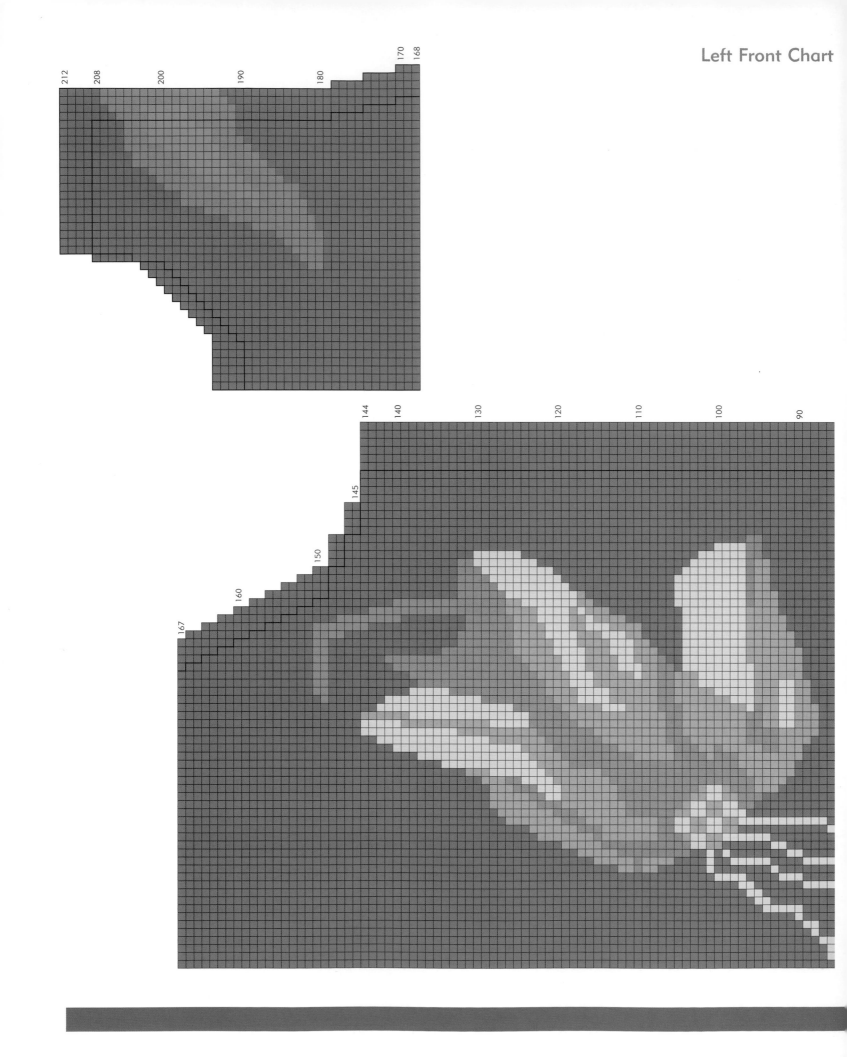

Color Key

- Excite (MC)
- Pick & Mix (A)
- Ivy (B)
- Candy Floss Pink (C)
- Dijon (D)
- Poppy (E)
- Oyster (F)
- Maritime (G)
- Pier (H)
- In the Pink (I)
- Tickle (J)

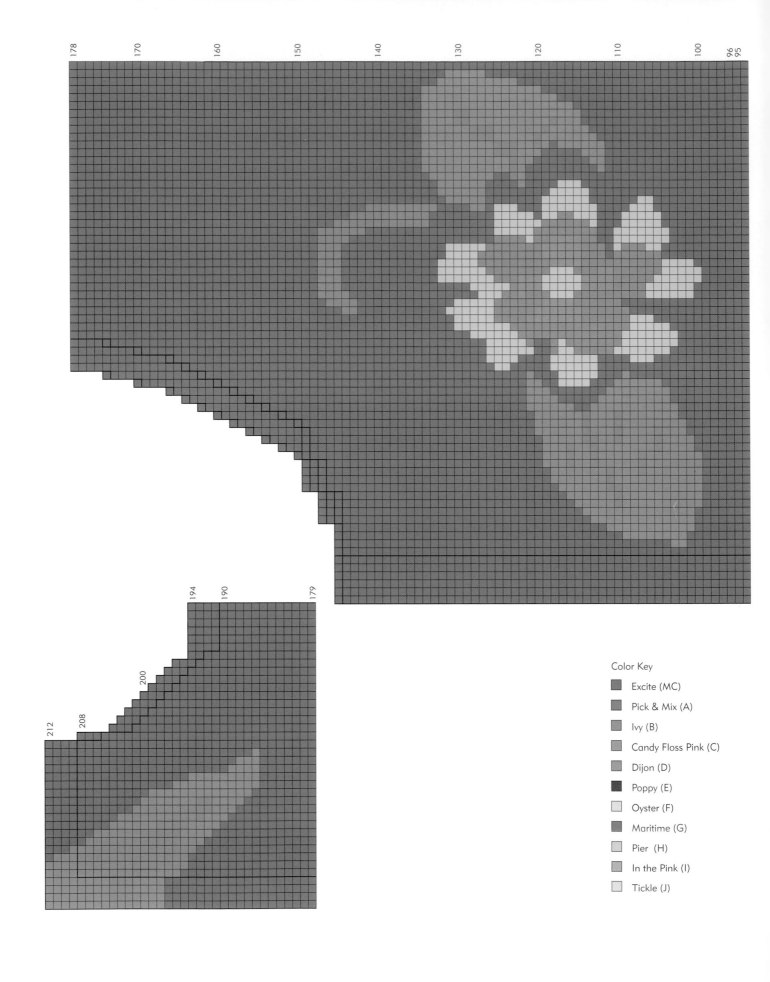

Color Key

■ Excite (MC)
■ Pick & Mix (A)
■ Ivy (B)
■ Candy Floss Pink (C)
■ Dijon (D)
■ Poppy (E)
□ Oyster (F)
■ Maritime (G)
□ Pier (H)
■ In the Pink (I)
□ Tickle (J)

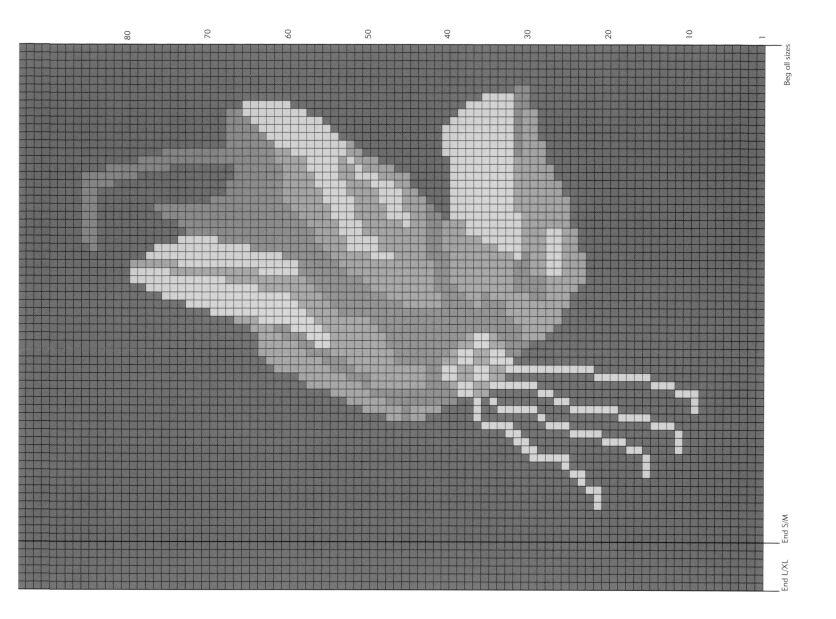

80 · 70 · 60 · 50 · 40 · 30 · 20 · 10 · 1

End S/M

End L/XL

Right Front Chart

End XS/S

End M/L

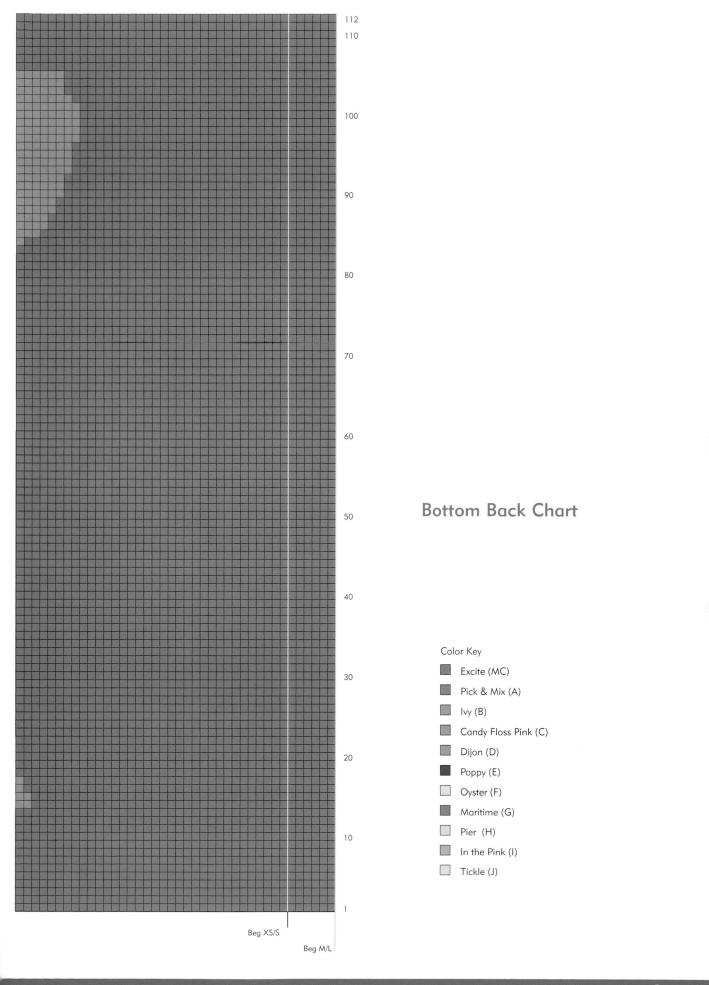

Bottom Back Chart

Color Key

- Excite (MC)
- Pick & Mix (A)
- Ivy (B)
- Candy Floss Pink (C)
- Dijon (D)
- Poppy (E)
- Oyster (F)
- Maritime (G)
- Pier (H)
- In the Pink (I)
- Tickle (J)

Beg XS/S

Beg M/L

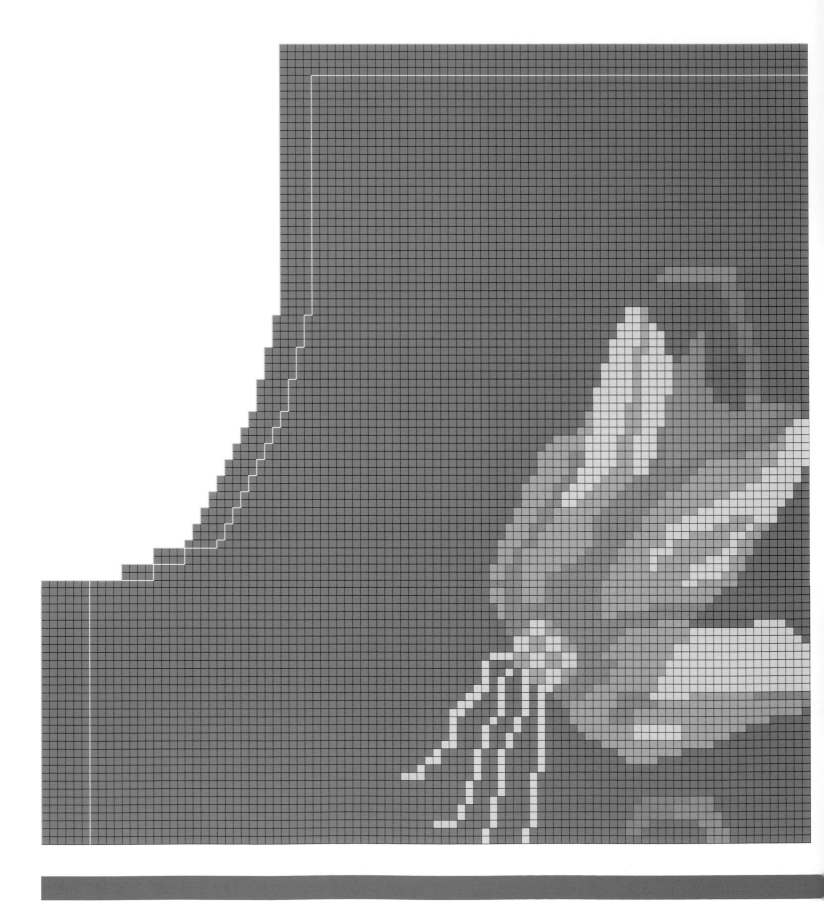

Top Back Chart

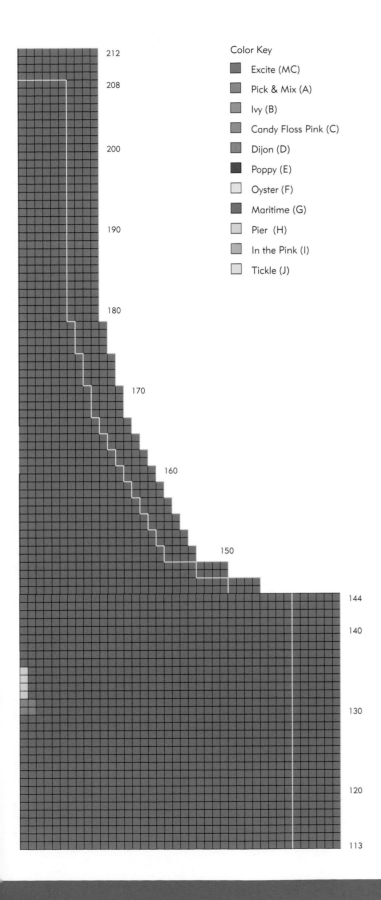

Color Key

- Excite (MC)
- Pick & Mix (A)
- Ivy (B)
- Candy Floss Pink (C)
- Dijon (D)
- Poppy (E)
- Oyster (F)
- Maritime (G)
- Pier (H)
- In the Pink (I)
- Tickle (J)

Child's Bird Vest

Materials

- 7 (7, 8) 1¾oz/50g balls (each approx 126yd/115m) of Rowan Yarns Cotton Glace (cotton) in #809 pier (MC)

- 1 (1, 2) balls in #815 excite (A)

- 1 ball each in #814 shoot (B), #816 mocha choc (C), #795 butter (D), #812 ivy (E), #741 poppy (F), #817 maritime (G), and #818 hot lips (H)

- One pair each sizes 4 and 6 (3.5 and 4mm) needles OR SIZE TO OBTAIN GAUGE

- Size 4 (3.5mm) circular needle, 16"/40cm long

- Bobbins

- Stitch holders

- Stitch markers

Sizes

Instructions are written for children's size 8. Changes for 10 and 12 are in parentheses.

Finished Measurements

- Chest 32 (34, 36)"/81 (86.5, 91.5)cm

- Length 17 (17½, 18)"/43 (44.5, 45.5)cm

Gauge

23 sts and 32 rows to 4"/10cm over St st and chart pat using larger needles.

TAKE TIME TO CHECK YOUR GAUGE.

Notes

1 When changing colors, pick up new color from under dropped color to prevent holes.

2 When working color rib pat or working over 1"/2.5cm or less of sts, carry color not in use loosely across WS of work.

3 For all other knitting, do not carry colors across. Use a separate bobbin of color for each color section.

4 Keep color changes on WS side of work.

COLOR RIB PATTERN

(multiple of 4 sts plus 2)

Row 1 (RS) K4 with A, *p2 with MC, k4 with A; rep from * to end.

Row 2 P4 with A, *k2 with MC, p4 with A; rep from * to end.

Rep rows 1 and 2 for color rib pat.

BACK

With smaller needles and A, cast on 94 (98, 106) sts. Work in color rib pat for 1"/2.5cm, end with a WS row. Change to larger needles. Cont in St st and work chart pat, beg and end as indicated. Work even through row 74, end with a WS row.

Armhole shaping

Bind off 5 sts at beg of next 2 rows. Dec 1 st each side every row 8 times—68 (72, 80) sts. Work even through row 128 (132, 136), end with a WS row. Cont with MC only.

Shoulder shaping

Bind off 20 (20, 24) sts at beg of next 2 rows. Place rem 28 (32, 32) sts on holder for back neck.

FRONT

Work as for back through row 86—68 (72, 80) sts.

Neck shaping

Row 87 (RS) K 33 (35, 39) sts, place rem 35 (37, 41) sts on holder for right front.

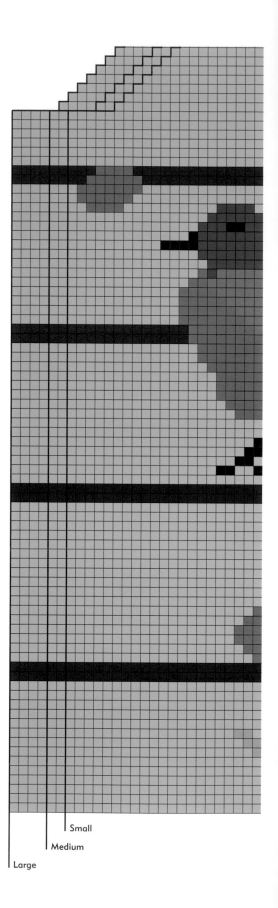

Color Key

- Pier (MC)
- Excite (A)
- Shoot (B)
- Mocha Choc (C)
- Butter (D)
- Ivy (E)
- Poppy (F)
- Maritime (G)
- Hot Lips (H)

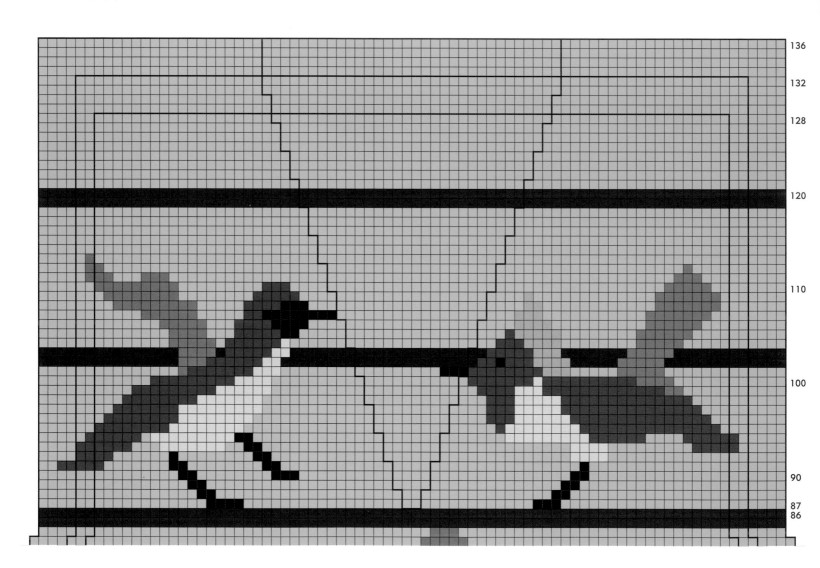

Row 88 Purl to end. Dec 1 st from neck edge on next row, then every 3rd row 12 (14, 14) times more—20 (20, 24) sts. Work even through row 128 (132, 136). Bind off. Place sts from holder back to LH needle.

Next row (RS) Place center 2 sts on holder, join yarn, k to end.

Next row Purl to end. Cont to work as left front, reversing all shaping.

FINISHING

Block pieces to measurements. Sew right shoulder seam.

Neckband

With RS facing, smaller needles and MC, pick up and k 44 (48, 52) sts evenly spaced along left front neck, pm, k2 sts from front neck holder, pm, pick up and k 44 (48, 52) sts along right front neck, k 28 (32, 32) sts from back neck holder—118 (130, 138) sts. Beg with row 2, work in color rib pat for 1 row.

Dec row 1 Work in color rib pat to 2 sts before first marker, p2tog, sl marker, k2, sl marker, p2tog, work in rib to end. Work in color rib pat as established for 1 row.

Dec row 2 Work in color rib pat to 2 sts before first marker, ssk, sl marker, k2, sl marker, k2tog, work in rib to end. Work in color rib pat as established for 1 more row. Bind off all sts loosely in color rib pat. Sew left shoulder and neckband seams.

Armbands

With RS facing, smaller needles and MC, pick up and k 106 (114, 122) sts evenly spaced along armhole edge. Beg with row 2, work in color rib pat for 4 rows. Bind off loose in color rib pat. Sew side and armband seams.

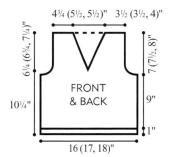

6¼ (6¾, 7¼)"
4¾ (5½, 5½)" 3½ (3½, 4)"
7 (7½, 8)"
10¼"
FRONT & BACK
9"
1"
16 (17, 18)"

India

Of all my travels, what is the most inspiring place? It is difficult to say, as each place offers such an individual flavor. But of the many countries I have visited worldwide, my mind's eye always turns back to India.

Why India? I suppose it is because of the simplicity of life there, the way that poor people use extravagant amounts of color in both their dress and on their buildings, as if to lift their spirits and make them feel good—as colors do. They use color fearlessly in everyday life, from clothing to simple displays of fruit in the market to their famous handcrafts and textiles.

With every blink of my eyes I got a thrill in this amazing country, from vibrant saris stacked on the market stalls, to goat herders striding country roads with carefully balanced bundles of sticks on their heads. Pastel-colored buildings sport life-

sized painted tigers and elephants. Opulently carved Hindu temples are decorated in vivid hues. (Some of these impressions of India's riotous use of color are captured for you to enjoy in a video called "Kaffe's Colour Quest." The video also includes a trip to Vietnam and a tour of the Kaffe Fassett Studio in London.)

I was struck by the intense color of India on my first trip there, when I was invited to assist on a project through the international charity Oxfam. Our mission was to help weavers produce work that would find a market in the West. Our main stop in Southern India was miles from the nearest town, a place that did not seem to exist on a map.

The villages consisted of a cluster of huts made from sticks — some of which had begun to sprout new growth. Layered banana leaves made up the roofs.

The women, who seemed to do all the hard labor, walked around in elegantly colored saris that starkly contrasted with the barren landscape. The men wore sarong-type garments appropriate for the intense heat.

As a treat for the children of the village, I filled our Jeep with an assortment of colored balloons. This caused a frenzy of excitement as

Clockwise from top: Weavers working on Kaffe Fassett fabrics; family resting by a decorated storefront; knitted swatch designs for weavers to work from; marketplace fashions.

we drove back into the village. I felt like the Pied Piper. The hours of ecstatic joy caused by this simple treat spoke volumes.

I stopped in one area to visit the weekly market where sellers gather from all over. Patchwork quilts made of shimmering fabrics were strung on clotheslines along with hand-painted bed sheets. Handmade sequined shoes and silver jewelry were everywhere—the assortment was overwhelming. A display of shimmering Lurex tops called out to me, its layout of squares in hot colors winking at me in the sunlight .

I combined the Rowan Summer Tweed yarns with Rowan Lurex Shimmer to capture the color palette for my Squares Jacket. Then I used the same color mood to create a felted bag. I also couldn't resist throwing in the striped knitted stole I'd done for *Vogue Knitting* in the past, as it is such a celebration piece and a real homage to the inspiration India has fed me through my visits. This piece saw me through years of workshops—I used the yarn scraps left over from a class. The piece is approximately 180 stitches wide on a US 3 (3.25mm) needle and approximately 7 feet long. The effort of working this on such a fine needle adds to the elegant drape.

Clockwise from bottom left: Colorful bangles; a man selling fabric; a beachcomber selling food; fresh mangos at a local market; woman keeping cool in the noontime heat.

Squares Jacket

Materials

- 3 1¾oz/50g hanks (each approx 118yd/108m) of Rowan Yarns Summer Tweed (cotton) in #523 legend (A)

- 1 hank each in #512 exotic (B), #527 sprig (C), #528 brilliant (D), #539 vanity (E), #538 butter ball (F), #507 rush (G), #536 torrid (H), and #510 bouquet (I)

- 1 .87oz/25g ball (each approx 104yd/95m) of Rowan Yarns Lurex Shimmer (viscose/polyester) each in #336 gleam (J) and #332 antique white gold (K)

- One pair each sizes 6 and 8 (4 and 5mm) needles OR SIZE TO OBTAIN GAUGE

- Bobbins

- Six ⅝"/16mm buttons

Size

One size fits most.

Finished Measurements

- Bust (closed) 49"/124.5cm

- Length 25"/63.5cm

- Upper arm 20"/51cm

Gauge

16 sts and 22 rows to 4"/10cm over St st and chart pat using larger needles.

TAKE TIME TO CHECK YOUR GAUGE.

Notes

1 Some color blocks are worked with one strand of Summer Tweed held tog with one strand of Lurex Shimmer. All other color blocks are worked with one strand of Summer Tweed only.

2 Do not carry colors across; use a separate bobbin of color for each color section.

3 When changing colors, pick up new color from under dropped color to prevent holes.

4 Keep color changes on WS side of work.

BACK

With smaller needles and A, cast on 99 sts. Work in garter st for 4 rows. Change to larger needles. Keeping 3 sts each side edge in garter st and A for side slits, and rem sts in St st, work chart beg and end as indicated through row 20. Cont to work all sts in St st and work through row 148. Bind off all sts.

LEFT FRONT

With smaller needles and A, cast on 49 sts. Work in garter st for 4 rows. Change to larger needles. Keeping 3 sts at side edge in garter st and A for side slit, and rem sts in St st, work chart beg and end as indicated through row 20. Cont to work all sts in St st and work through row 129.

Neck shaping

Row 130 (WS) Bind off 8 sts, work to end. Dec 1 st at neck edge every row 8 times—33 sts. Work even through row 148. Bind off.

RIGHT FRONT

With smaller needles and A, cast on 49 sts. Work in garter st for 4 rows. Change to larger needles. Keeping 3 sts at side edge in garter st and A for side slit, and rem sts in St st, work chart beg and end as indicated through row 20. Cont to work all sts in St st and work through row 128. Cont to shape neck as for left front, reversing all shaping.

SLEEVES

With smaller needles and A, cast on 41 sts. Work in garter st for 4 rows. Change to larger needles. Cont in St st and work chart, beg and end as indicated. AT THE SAME TIME, inc 1 st each side every 5th row 20 times—81 sts. Work even through row 105. Bind off all sts purlwise.

FINISHING

Block pieces to measurements. Sew shoulder seams.

Button band

With RS facing, smaller needles and A, pick up and k 97 sts evenly spaced along left front edge. Work in garter st for 4 rows. Bind off all sts loosely knitwise. Place markers for 6 buttons on button band, with the first 4"/10cm from lower edge, the last 1"/2.5cm from neck edge and the others evenly spaced between.

Buttonhole band

With RS facing, smaller needles and A, pick up and k 97 sts evenly spaced along right front edge. Knit next row. **Buttonhole row (RS)** *K to marker, yo, k2tog; rep from * 5 times more. Cont in garter st for 2 rows. Bind off all sts loosely knitwise.

Collar

With RS facing, smaller needles and A, pick up and k 86 sts evenly spaced along neck edge, beg after buttonhole band and ending before button band. Work even in garter st for 3½"/9cm. Bind off all sts loosely knitwise. Place markers 10"/25.5cm down from shoulders on back and fronts. Sew sleeves to armholes between markers. Sew side seams leaving bottom 3½"/9cm open for side slits. Sew sleeve seams. Sew on buttons.

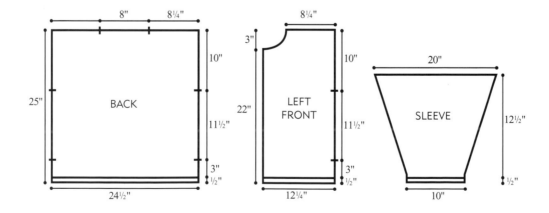

India 86/87

Color Key

- ■ Legend (A)
- ■ Exotic (B)
- ■ Sprig (C)
- ■ Brilliant (D)
- ■ Vanity (E)
- ■ Butter Ball (F)
- ■ Rush (G)
- ■ Torrid (H)
- ■ Bouquet (I)
- △ Gleam (J) held tog with Summer Tweed
- ◎ Antique White Gold (K) held tog

  with Summer Tweed

- — Knit on WS rows

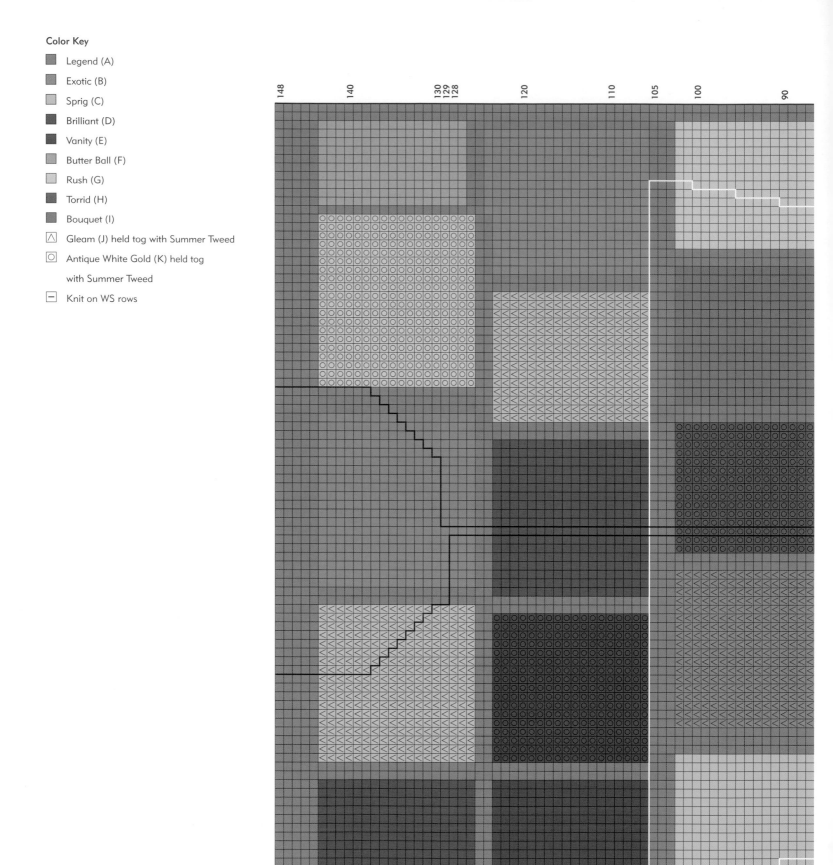

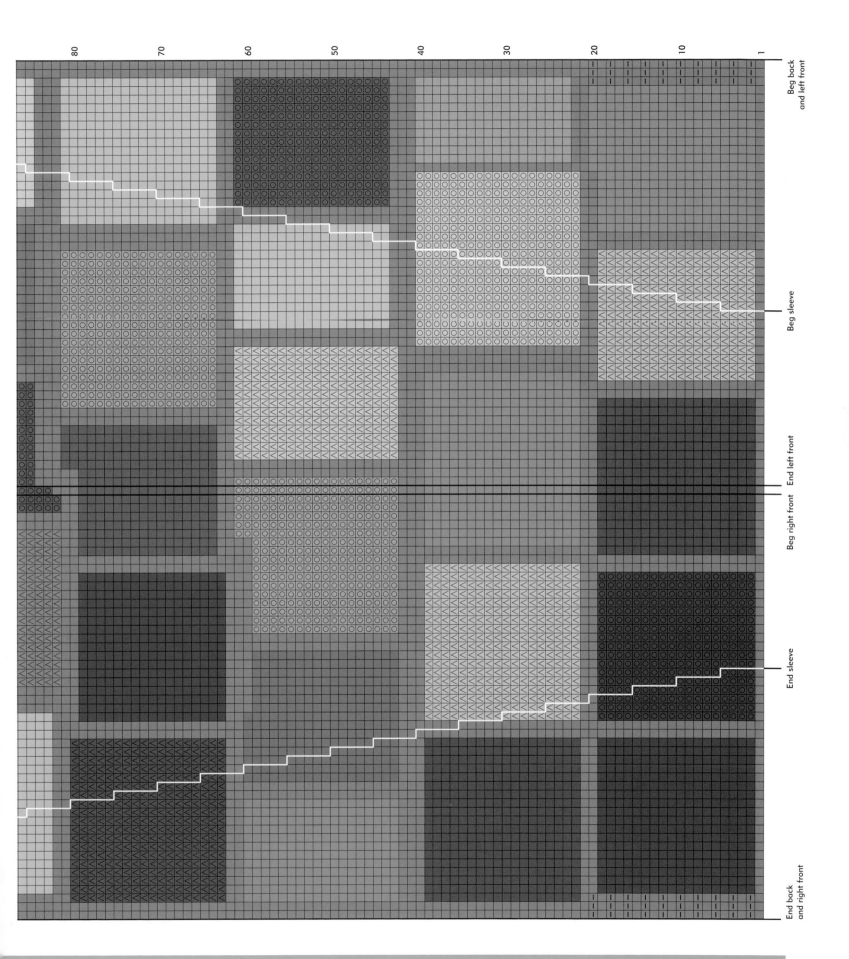

Squares Bag

Materials

- 2 1¾oz/50g balls (each approx 124yd/113m) of Rowan Yarns Scottish Tweed DK (wool) in #19 peat (A)

- 1 ball each in #17 lobster (B), #3 skye (C), #18 thatch (D), #11 sunset (E) and #4 storm grey (F)

- One pair size 9 (5.5mm) needles OR SIZE TO OBTAIN GAUGE

- Bobbins

Finished Measurements

- 8" x 10"/20.5 x 25.5cm (after felting and excluding strap)

Gauge

16 sts and 23 rows to 4"/10cm over St st using size 9 (5.5mm) needles and 2 strands of yarn held tog (before felting).

TAKE TIME TO CHECK YOUR GAUGE.

Notes

1 Use 2 strands of yarn held tog throughout.

2 Back and front of bag are made from side to side.

3 Do not carry colors across; use a separate bobbin of color for each color section.

4 When changing colors, pick up new color from under dropped color to prevent holes.

5 Keep color changes on WS side of work.

BACK

Beg at side edge, with 2 strands of A held tog, cast on 48 sts. Knit next 4 rows.

Beg color pat

Row 1 (RS) K4 with A, k18 with B, k4 with A, k18 with C, k4 with A.

Row 2 P4 with A, p18 with C, p4 with A, p18 with B, p4 with A.

Rows 3-18 Rep rows 1 and 2.

Row 19 With A, knit.

Row 20 With A, purl.

Row 21 K4 with A, k18 with D, k4 with A, k18 with E, k4 with A.

Row 22 P4 with A, p18 with E, p4 with A, p18 with D, p4 with A.

Rows 23–38 Rep rows 21 and 22.

Rows 39 and 40 Rep rows 19 and 20.

Row 41 K4 with A, k18 with F, k4 with A, k18 with B, k4 with A.

Row 42 P4 with B, p18 with C, p4 with F, p18 with B, p4 with A.

Rows 43–58 Rep rows 41 and 42. Knit next 4 rows. Bind off all sts loosely.

FRONT

Work as for back.

STRAP

With 2 strands of A held tog, cast on 6 sts. Work in k1, p1 rib for 45"/114.5cm. Bind off all sts loosely in rib.

FINISHING

Sew side and bottom edges of bag tog leaving top edge open. On WS of bag, center one end of strap over a side seam, so short edge of strap is approx 2"/5cm from top edge of bag. Sew end of strap in place. Rep for opposite end of strap.

Felting

Fill washing machine to low water setting at a hot temperature. Add ¼ cup of a gentle detergent and 2 Tbs. of baking soda. Add bag and also a pair of jeans to provide abrasion and balanced agitation. Use 15-to 20-minute wash cycle, including cold rinse and spin. Check measurements of bag. If bag is still bigger than finished measurements, repeat process with progressively shorter cycles, measuring every few minutes until desired size is achieved. Air dry or machine-dry on a low setting. Steam block to finished measurements.

Striped Throw

Materials

■ Various 4-ply yarns and colors from Rowan Yarns

■ One pair size 3 (3.25mm) needles OR SIZE TO OBTAIN GAUGE

■ Size D/3 (3.25mm) crochet hook

Finished Measurements

■ Approx 27" x 84"/68.5cm x 213cm with edging

Gauge

28 sts and 40 rows to 4"/10cm over St st using size 3 (3.25mm) needles.

TAKE TIME TO CHECK YOUR GAUGE.

WRAP

Cast on 180 sts with desired color. Work in St st, working first and last st in garter st for selvage sts, using colors and yarns as desired, for 83"/211cm, or desired length. Bind off.

Edging

With RS facing, crochet hook and desired color, work evenly around entire outside edge as foll:

Next rnd *Sc, ch 1, skip 1 st (or row); rep from * evenly around outside edge, working (sc, ch 1, sc, ch 1) in each corner.

Next 3 rnds With desired color work sc, ch 1 in each ch-1 sp. Fasten off.

FINISHING

Weave in ends. Block to measurements.

Italy

I have had the good fortune of visiting Venice twice, and each time
I've had the strong feeling that I was stumbling onto a period film set
or into a classical painting.

All the buildings seem to have their own charm
and character, their harmonious colorings unifying
the city. It is a place where contemporary architecture, neon lights, and brash colors do not exist.
I can still remember my sigh of delight as I entered
this magical city, brimming with mystery and
character. I can see the narrow walkways between
canals; the terra-cotta and stone buildings five
stories high, with their long, wooden shutters; the
walls painted soft earthy tones, from deep ocher to

faded pink; the ancient weathered patinas. Ladies in aprons lower baskets from the top-floor windows to hoist up their groceries. Laundry lines strung high across the narrow alleyways billow like huge flags. Grand buildings boast large wooden doorways with heavily carved frames and steps leading to the waterways, lending another edge of mystery and intrigue.

The city is split by the twisting Grand Canal, fringed by red-and-white-striped poles that seem to have become a symbol of the city. The waterways are bustling with sleek black gondolas, wooden barges, and vaporettos carrying varied wares, from heavy machinery to crates of vegetables and bottles of wine. Water taxis take the place of cars as they pass under splendid humpbacked bridges and wind their way through enchanting canals. Somehow, all of these intertwining waterways seem to lead to the heart of Venice: St. Mark's Square. St. Mark's is a grand piazza fringed with columned alleyways and cafés that spill out onto the cobblestones. On one side is the Doge's Palace, a stunning marble building supported by a colonnade of arches and columns. Next to it, at the end of the square, sits the famous St. Mark's Basilica, its opulent crescent-shaped entrance encrusted in

From left to right: Magnificently colored mosaic entrance to St. Mark's Basilica, Venice; cafés along the piazza.

mosaics in rich royal blues, reds, and gold. The floors in the cathedral's vast interior are decorated with geometric patterns made of marble, and towering columns lead up to gold mosaic ceilings. Kaffe, with whom I visited this magnificent structure, remarked, "How people concentrate on praying in such a visual building, I don't know!" While my first trip to Venice was purely a vacation, my second trip was to fulfill a dream of Kaffe's: to find a delicate Venetian chandelier covered in glass flowers for a room he had painted. The design was his version of Chinese wallpaper, painted in soft greens with voluptuous peonies. After hunting the antique shops in London and Paris for the right chandelier, we decided to come to Venice. The Missoni family lent us their rooftop vacation apartment overlooking the city, giving us a wonderful base. We headed out to the island of Murano, the center of Venetian glassmaking. This intimate island is a maze of back streets leading off the main canal, each street lined with showrooms housing floor after floor of shimmering light fixtures. (I, for one, would hate to do the dusting in these places!) Despite all of this variety, however, Kaffe never found the chandelier he had in mind. We finally came across a workshop where he worked with a glassblower to design a classical Venetian chandelier to his own specifications. It works perfectly in his room, and he now wants to design more of them.

My own design inspiration comes from the brickwork on the Doge's Palace, whose elegant design cried out to me as a natural Fair Isle pattern. In my St. Mark's Jacket, I tried to recreate this pattern using the soft chalky pastels of the stone throughout the city. If the palette is a little pale for your taste, try a rich periwinkle-blue for the main body color, a taupe for the lattice, and maybe a darker blue or chocolate-brown for the alcove. I get such a thrill seeing what others come up with, especially if they work in colors they are comfortable with. When in doubt, knit a swatch to see how your color choices work together before starting the garment.

Clockwise from bottom left: Reflections in the waters of Venice; laundry hanging like bunting flags; Doge's Palace with its creamy pastel brickwork.

St. Mark's Jacket

Materials

- 12 (13, 14) 1¾oz/50g balls (each approx 186yd/170m) of Rowan Yarns 4 Ply Cotton (cotton) in #112 opaque (A)

- 7 (8, 8) balls in #120 orchid (B)

- 2 (3, 3) balls in #136 bluebell (C)

- 1 .87oz/25g ball (approx 120yd/110m) of Rowan Yarns Yorkshire Tweed 4 Ply (wool) in #263 desiccated (D)

- One pair each sizes 4 and 6 (3.5 and 4mm) needles OR SIZE TO OBTAIN GAUGE

- Bobbins

- Seven ⅝"/16mm buttons

Sizes

Instructions are written for size Small. Changes for Medium and Large are in parentheses.

Finished Measurements

- Bust (closed) 39 (42, 45)"/99 (106.5, 114.5)cm

- Length 25½ (26, 26½)"/64.5 (66, 67.5)cm

- Upper arm 18 (19, 20)"/45.5 (48, 51)cm

Gauges

24 sts and 27 rows to 4"/10cm over St st and chart pats 1, 2 and 4 using larger needles and 2 strands of yarn held tog.

26 sts and 28 rows to 4"/10cm over St st and chart pat 3 using larger needles and 2 strands of yarn held tog.

TAKE TIME TO CHECK YOUR GAUGE.

Heading out of Lima is like passing through a garden gate. Since the rainy season had just passed, the hillsides and fields were alive with every possible shade of green. Even the new seedlings in the farm fields made the rich brown earth look like a luminous shot cotton. Deeper in the countryside, young girls appeared from nowhere, dressed in woven garments in shades of hot red. With their black hair they looked adorable, like bundles of freshly picked poppies.

South America is known for its fine hand-knitting. One of the working relationships of which we are most proud is with a knitwear company called Peruvian Connection. They produce a handsome range of pima cotton and hand-knitted alpaca garments that they sell through their mail-order catalog. Kaffe has contributed many garments to this company, so visiting the knitters in Peru was a real treat. Since Kaffe uses dozens of colors in each garment, it takes the knitters there a week just to weave in the ends.

Flying into Cuzco, high in the mountains, takes your breath away because of the extreme altitude. From Cuzco we took a small train to the extraordinary ruins of the Inca city of Machu Picchu, which is perched on the narrow camel's back of a precipice. It is staggering how this magical place came about. Each massive steely gray unit of stone is perfectly cut and placed like a massive jigsaw puzzle. One wonders how this was done when modern tools were not available.

Choosing between the high contrast this country presents, from the dramatic landscapes to the rich colors of its textiles, I have taken as my inspiration this deep, earthy palette. This is an easy color scheme to wear, especially for men who prefer a more tame wardrobe. The pattern also knits up beautifully as a pillow or throw, if you want an easier project.

Clockwise from bottom left: Gorgeously bright parrots stand out against tiled roofs; a scene from the market; stunning stone architecture of Macchu Picchu; exotic fruit stacked high on brightly colored tablecloths.

Peruvian Vest

Materials

- 2 (2, 3) .87oz/25g balls (each approx 120yd/110m) of Rowan Yarns Scottish Tweed 4 Ply (wool) in #14 heath (A)

- 1 (1, 2) ball each in #16 thistle (B), #9 rust (C), #13 claret (D), #20 mallard (E), #17 lobster (F), #22 celtic mix (G), #19 peat (H), #12 wine (I), #8 herring (J), and #23 midnight (K)

- One pair size 3 (3.25mm) needles OR SIZE TO OBTAIN GAUGE

- Size 3 (3.25mm) circular needle, 16"/40cm long

- Bobbins

- Stitch holders

- Stitch markers

Sizes

Instructions are written for Men's size Small. Changes for Medium and Large are in parentheses.

Finished Measurements

- Chest 40 (44, 48)"/101.5 (111.5, 122)cm

- Length 23 (24, 25)"/58.5 (61, 63.5)cm

Gauge

28 sts and 40 rows to 4"/10cm over St st and chart pat using size 3 (3.25mm) needles.

TAKE TIME TO CHECK YOUR GAUGE.

Notes

1 Do not carry colors across; use a separate bobbin of color for each color section.

2 When changing colors, pick up new color from under dropped color to prevent holes.

3 Keep color changes on WS side of work.

K2, P2 RIB

(multiple of 4 sts plus 2)

Row 1 (RS) K2, *p2, k2; rep from * to end.

Row 2 P2, *k2, p2; rep from * to end.

Rep rows 1 and 2 for k2, p2 rib.

BACK

With A, cast on 142 (154, 170) sts. Working in k2, p2 rib, work in stripe pat as folls: 2 rows A, 2 rows B, 2 rows A, 2 rows C, 2 rows A, 2 rows D, 2 rows A, 2 rows E and 2 rows A. Cont in St st and work chart pat, beg and end as indicated. Work through row 56, then rep rows 1-56

until piece measures 14 (14½, 15)"/35.5 (37, 38)cm from beg, end with a WS row.

Armhole shaping

Bind off 9 (10, 11) sts at beg of next 2 rows. Dec 1 st each side every row twice, then every other row 7 (9, 11) times—106 (112, 122) sts. Work even until armhole measures 9 (9½, 10)"/23 (24, 25.5)cm, end with a WS row.

Shoulder shaping

Bind off 28 (30, 34) sts at beg of next 2 rows. Place rem 50 (52, 54) sts on holder for back neck.

FRONT

Work as for back to armhole shaping.

Armhole and neck shaping

Bind off 9 (10, 11) sts at beg of next 2 rows. Dec 1 st each side every row twice—120 (130, 144) sts.

Next row (RS) K2tog, k until you have 56 (61, 68) sts on needle, k2tog, place rem 61 (66, 73) sts on holder for right front. Cont to dec 1

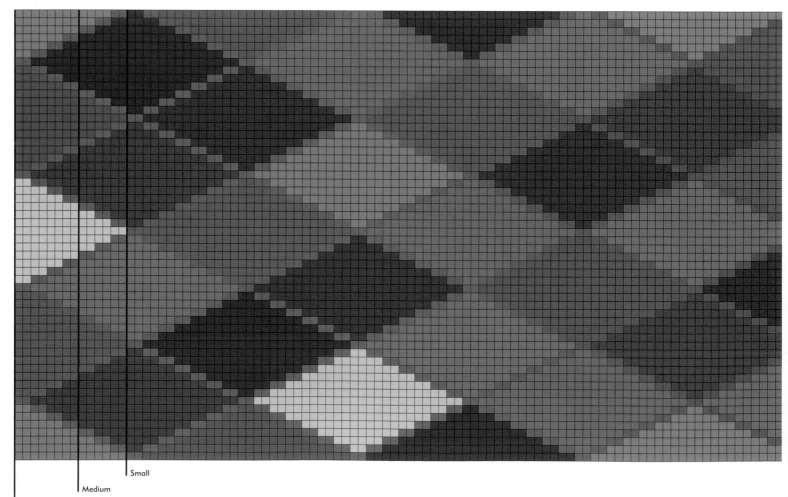

Small

Medium

Large

st from armhole edge every other row 6 (9, 10) times more. AT THE SAME TIME, cont to dec 1 st from neck edge every 3rd row 23 (24, 25) times more. Work even on 28 (30, 34) sts until piece measures same length as back to shoulder, end with a WS row. Bind off. Place sts from holder back to LH needle.

Next row (RS) Place center 2 sts on holder, join yarn, k2tog, work to last 2 sts, k2tog. Cont to work as left front, reversing all shaping.

FINISHING

Block pieces to measurements. Sew shoulder seams.

Neckband

With RS facing, circular needle and A, pick up and k 48 (53, 56) sts evenly spaced along left front neck, pm, k2 sts from front neck holder, pm, pick up and k 48 (53, 56) sts along right front neck, k 50 (52, 54) sts from back neck holder—148 (160, 168) sts. Join and pm to indicate beg of rnds. Work in k2, p2 rib for 1 rnd.

Next (dec) rnd Work in rib to 2 sts before first marker, ssk, sl marker, k2, sl marker, k2tog, work in rib to end. Rep this rnd 8 times more. AT

THE SAME TIME, work in stripe pat as folls: 2 rnds E, 2 rnds A, 2 rnds D and 2 rnds A. Bind off all sts loosely using A.

Armbands

With RS facing and A, pick up and k 122 (130, 138) sts evenly spaced along armhole edge. Beg with row 2, work in k2, p2 rib for 2 rows. Cont in stripe pat as folls: 1 row D, 1 row A, 1 row E and 2 rows A. Bind off all sts loosely in rib using A. Sew side and armband seams.

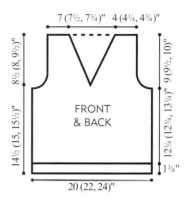

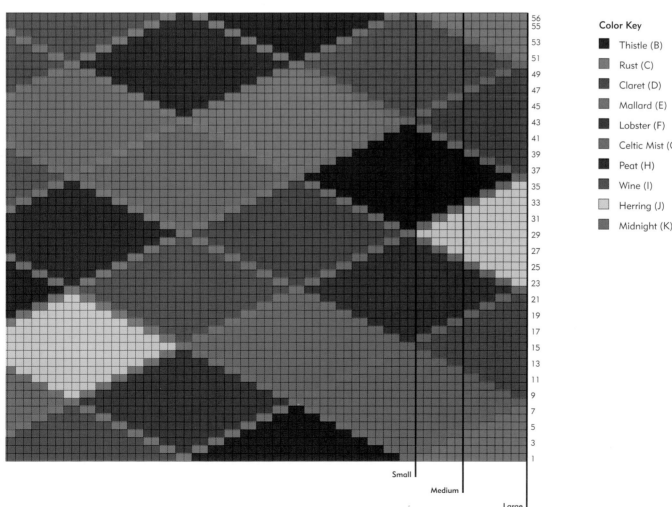

Color Key
- Thistle (B)
- Rust (C)
- Claret (D)
- Mallard (E)
- Lobster (F)
- Celtic Mist (G)
- Peat (H)
- Wine (I)
- Herring (J)
- Midnight (K)

Small
Medium
Large

South Africa

From the moment I set foot on South African soil, my trip was memorable. We were greeted by the wife of the chief of the Ndebele tribe, who was draped in a bold striped blanket of maroon, yellow, and cobalt.

Her round, shaved head was framed in a crown of white beads decorated with gold coins. Her neck was braced with a stack of brass bands, as if supporting her chin. I asked if she ever removed these bands. "No, these are my wedding bands," she replied. Around her waist were pale-blue and dusty pink beads, and fat bangles of the same style covered her ankles over rings of gold that went up to her knees. Her dainty white tennis shoes were her only concession to Western dress.

We drove northwest of the city across a barren landscape to visit her village. We had been on the road for over two hours when an advance party of blanket-clad, bright-bereted ladies suddenly appeared, dancing up the road while singing and

blowing whistles to announce our arrival at the chief's house. His home was a humble bungalow, but it was decorated in the most brave graphic patterns of black lines with red and yellow set on white backgrounds. Every inch was painted immaculately as if done yesterday— including the yard wall. This was the same color palette depicted in their beadwork, which they were proud to show us. We were offered a ceremonial lunch of their favorite food, brought in especially for their honored guests: stone cold Kentucky Fried Chicken and fries.

A week later at a famous Crossroads township in Cape Town, we found rows of patchwork shacks constructed from sheets of weathered plywood, plastic, and corrugated metal. We were there to host workshops with people from the townships, to encourage their craft skills. At the center of the shacks, we found a workshop that handprinted T-shirts and tablecloths. The crowd in the studio was a bit withdrawn, so out of the blue I asked if anyone could sing. There was a shy silence, followed by some whispers. Then the roof blew off.

From left to right: Homes along a South African hillside; a riot of color on beach huts.

They sang with gusto and danced around the room. After a few songs, they settled down and worked in total harmony. Inspired by this event, I now ask people to sing in my workshops in other countries.

The people of South Africa have a flawless and original sense of placement that is evident in the work that pours out of the continent. In Durban, there is an art center called the BAT Centre, every inch decorated in mosaic, collage, and murals. The shop specializes in selling the art of local craftspeople who live close to the poverty line in the township, encouraging them to continue to create their work. They sell items like baskets made from colorful telephone wires, hooked rugs, ceramics, beadwork, and miniature painted clay masks.

We attended the famous arts festival in the small picturesque mountain town called Grahamstown, between Johannesburg and Cape Town. During the

festival week, street performers, music, and art seemed to ooze out from every corner. A painted bus stop grabbed my attention. Decorated in jolly clown faces on a rich royal blue background, it made me think of the mood colors of a Kandinsky canvas. But it was a garbage can, painted by children from a local school in canary-yellow with random colorful handprints, that prompted me to knit three pillows using a similar motif. I toned down the colors and placed the handprint on a wide-striped background. I also designed a throw inspired by a piece of African beadwork. Both designs first appeared in the UK's *Knitting* magazine.

From left to right: A bus stop decorated in joyful colors; baskets woven out of telephone wires; a shantytown home with fruit carton packaging for wallpaper; a waste can painted by local children.

Diamond Throw

Materials

- 1 3½oz/100g ball (each approx 109yd/100m) of Rowan Yarns Plaid (wool/acrylic/alpaca) each in #156 hearty (A), #154 spicy (B) and #168 stormy night (C)

- 4 .87oz/25g balls (each approx 120yd/110m) of Rowan Yarns Scottish Tweed 4 Ply (wool) each in #00003 skye and #00011 sunset worked together (D); and #00010 brilliant pink and #00005 lavender worked together (E)

- 2 1¾oz/50g balls (each approx 123yd/113m) of Rowan Yarns Wool Cotton (merino wool/cotton) each in #00035 green olive (F), #00013 claret (G), and #00016 thistle (H)

- Size 11 (8mm) circular needle, 24"/60cm long OR SIZE TO OBTAIN GAUGE

- Size K/10½ (6.5mm) crochet hook

- Bobbins

Finished Measurements

- 41" x 40¼"/104 x 102cm

Gauge

13 sts and 16 rows to 4"/10cm over St st and charted pat using size 11 (8mm) needle.

TAKE TIME TO CHECK YOUR GAUGE.

Notes

1 Do not carry colors across; use a separate bobbin of color for each color section.

2 When changing colors, pick up new color from under dropped color to prevent holes.

3 Keep color changes on WS side of work.

THROW

With circular needle and A, cast on 135 sts. Do not join. Cont in St st and work rows 1–161 of chart. With A, bind off all sts purlwise.

FINISHING

Block piece to measurements.

Edging

With RS facing and crochet hook, join A with a sl st in any corner.

Rnd 1 Ch 1, making sure that work lies flat, sc evenly around entire edge working 2 sc in each corner. Join rnd with a sl st in first sc. Fasten off.

Color Key

Hearty (A)

Spicy (B)

Stormy Night (C)

Skye and Sunset (D)

Brilliant Pink and Lavender (E)

Green Olive (F)

Claret (G)

Thistle (H)

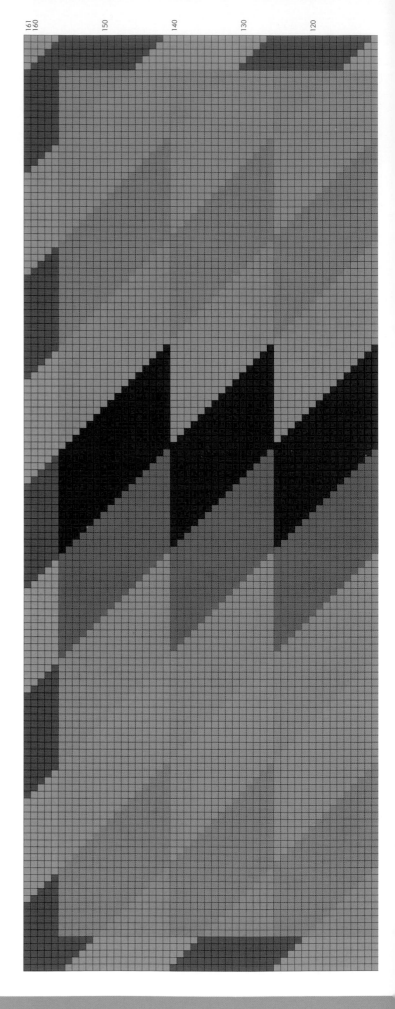

Hand Motif Pillows

Materials

Colorway I

■ 4 .87oz/25g balls (each approx 120yd/110m) of Rowan Yarns Scottish Tweed 4 Ply (wool) each in #16 thistle (A), #17 lobster (B), #12 wine (C), #15 apple (D), and #11 sunset (E)

Colorway II

■ 4 balls each in #4 storm grey (A), #6 seagreen (B), #8 herring (C), #23 midnight (D) and #24 porridge (E)

Colorway III

■ 4 balls each in #17 lobster (A), #18 thatch (B), #15 apple (C), #6 seagreen (D), and #3 skye (E)

■ One pair size 7 (4.5mm) needles OR SIZE TO OBTAIN GAUGE

■ Bobbins

■ Five ⅞"/22mm buttons

■ 14" x 17"/35.5 x 43cm pillow form

Finished Measurements

■ 14" x 17"/35.5 x 43cm

Gauge

19 sts and 26 rows to 4"/10cm over St st and chart pat using size 7 (4.5mm) needles and 2 strands held tog.

TAKE TIME TO CHECK YOUR GAUGE.

Notes

1 Use 2 strands of yarn held tog throughout.

2 Do not carry colors across; use a separate bobbin of color for each color section.

3 When changing colors, pick up new color from under dropped color to prevent holes.

4 Keep color changes on WS side of work.

FRONT (all colorways)

With A and B held tog, cast on 82 sts. Cont in St st and work rows 1-90 of chart. Bind off.

BACK (Colorways I and II)

Bottom half

With A and B held tog, cast on 81 sts. Cont in St st and stripe pat as folls: 12 rows A and B, 12 rows C, 12 rows A and B, 8 rows C. Cont with C only as folls:

Button band

Row 1 (RS) K3, *p2, k3; rep from * to end.

Row 2 P3, *k3, p3; rep from * to end. Rep these 2 rows twice more. Bind off all sts loosely in rib. Place markers for 5 buttons on button band, with the first and last 2"/5cm from side edges and the others evenly spaced between.

Top half

With 2 strands of C held tog, cast on 81 sts. Cont in St st and stripe pat as folls: [12 rows C, 12 rows A and B] twice. Cont with C only as folls:

Buttonhole band

Work in rib as for bottom half for 2 rows.

Buttonhole row (RS) *Work in rib to marker, yo, k2tog; rep from * 4 times more, work in rib to end. Cont in ribbing for 3 more rows. Bind off all sts loosely in rib.

BACK (Colorway III)

Bottom half

With 2 strands of C held tog, cast on 81 sts. Work in St st for 44 rows. Work buttonband as for bottom half of colorways I and II. Place markers for 5 buttons on button band, with the first and last 2"/5cm from side edges and the others evenly spaced between.

Top half

With 2 strands of A held tog, cast on 81 sts. Work in St st for 48 rows. Work buttonhole band as for top half of colorways I and II.

FINISHING

Block pieces to measurements. Lap back buttonhole band over button band; pin together along length of bands. With RS facing, sew front and back together around all edges. Remove pins. Turn RS out. Sew on buttons to correspond to buttonholes. Insert pillow form; button closed.

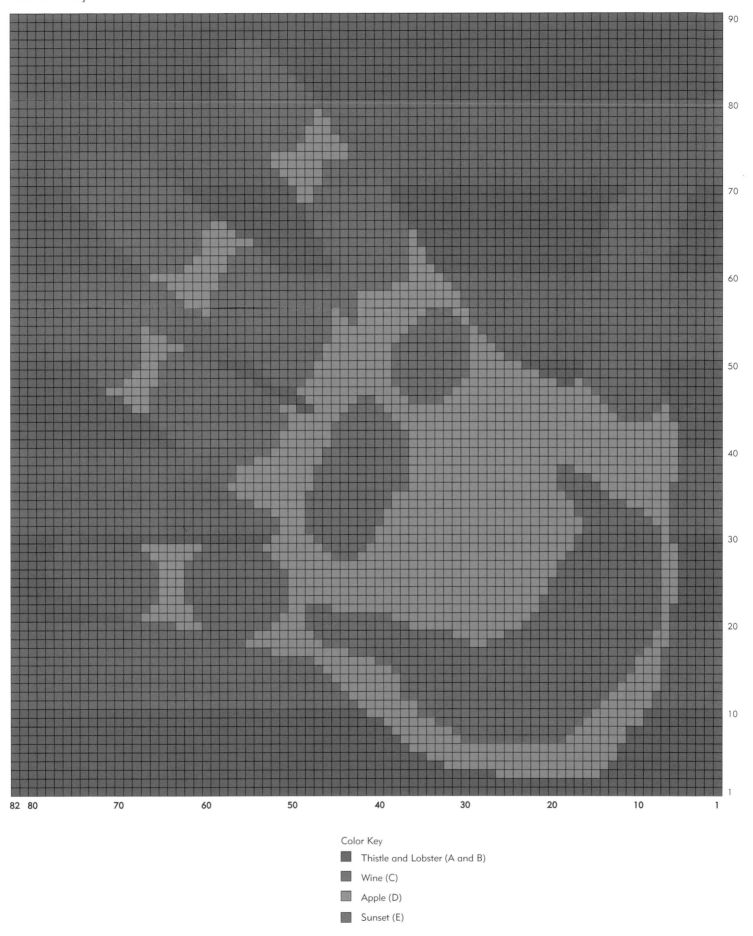

Color Key

- Thistle and Lobster (A and B)
- Wine (C)
- Apple (D)
- Sunset (E)

Colorway II

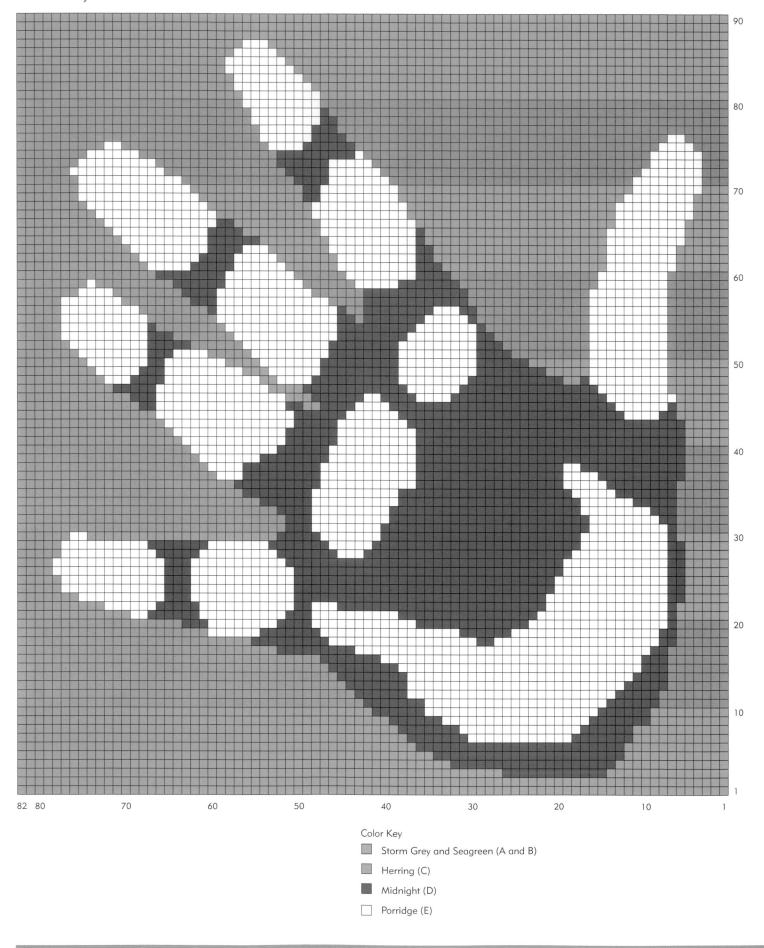

Color Key

■ Storm Grey and Seagreen (A and B)

■ Herring (C)

■ Midnight (D)

☐ Porridge (E)

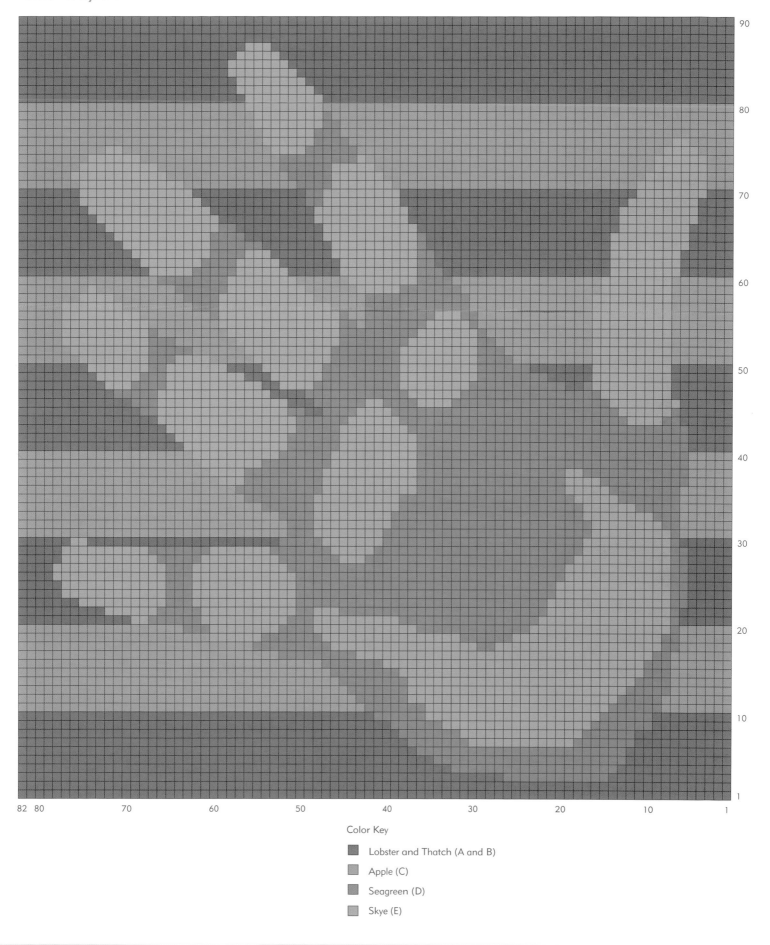

Color Key

■ Lobster and Thatch (A and B)
■ Apple (C)
■ Seagreen (D)
■ Skye (E)

United States

My first opportunity to visit the United States came when I was
offered a seasonal job working at a summer camp in Pennsylvania at
age 18. Arriving in New York City for an overnight stay, I found it hard
to contain my excitement.

I had never experienced anything on the scale of
those skyscrapers, and I remember having to strain
my neck just to see the sky. The next day, my
Greyhound bus left the city behind and rolled
through manicured farmland leading into the
Pocono Mountains. The bus dropped me off in the
historic small town of Honesdale, Pennsylvania,
where I was to live and work for the next six
months.

I worked that first summer as a kitchen hand, and I
returned the next year to take over the cook's job,
catering for 300 at a sitting. I spent the money I
earned experiencing firsthand what I had only seen
on TV. I took a bus from New York to San

Francisco, then down to San Diego and back. Traveling coast to coast on a non-stop, three-day journey filled me with wonder at the width and diversity of the country. I saw lush, open prairies; small towns where time seemed to stand still; built-up cities such as Chicago, with its gleaming, mirrored skyscrapers; barren mountainsides; and sweeping, scorched deserts leading to the lush greenery of western California.

Over the years, I have returned to the United States many times to give my "Color in Design" workshops. On all my visits—first as a wide-eyed young man and later as a seasoned traveler—I have had a wealth of experiences exploring new places. Highlights that come to mind are the charming towns in the Berkshires, the blazing colors of New Hampshire in the fall, and the leafy suburbs and grand houses of Little Rock, Arkansas. I have felt the exhilarating vibes of New York

Above: Fall colors on display throughout the United States.

Fire Maze Jacket

Materials

- 4 (6) 1¾ oz/50g balls (each approx 118yd/108m) of Rowan Yarns Summer Tweed (silk/cotton) in #537 summer berry (A)

- 4 balls in #536 torrid (B)

- 2 balls each in #515 raffia (C), #530 toast (D) and #500 power (E)

- One pair each sizes 7 and 8 (4.5 and 5mm) needles OR SIZE TO OBTAIN GAUGE

- Two each sizes 7 and 8 (4.5 and 5mm) circular needles, 24"/60cm long

- Bobbins

- Six ⅝"/16mm buttons

Sizes

Instructions are written for size Small/Medium. Changes for Large/X-Large are in parentheses.

Finished Measurements

- Chest (closed) 55 (61)"/139.5 (155)cm

- Length 26 (27)"/66 (68.5)cm

- Upper arm 22 (24)"/56 (61)cm

Gauge

18 sts and 24 rows to 4"/10cm over St st and chart pat using larger needles.

TAKE TIME TO CHECK YOUR GAUGE.

Notes

1 Do not carry colors across; use a separate bobbin of color for each color section.

2 When changing colors, pick up new color from under dropped color to prevent holes.

3 Keep color changes on WS side of work.

BACK

With smaller circular needle and B, cast on 124 (138) sts. Work back and forth using 2nd circular needle. Work in St st for 9 rows. Knit next row for turning ridge. Change to larger circular needles and A. Work even in St st for 0 (6) rows. Cont in St st and work chart I, beg and end as indicated. Work through row 20 (14). Mark beg and end of last row for beg of pocket openings. Work through row 48 (42). Mark beg and end of last row for end of pocket openings. Work through row 157. With A only, work 1 row more. Bind off.

RIGHT FRONT

With smaller needles and B, cast on 54 (61) sts. Work in St st for 9 rows, inc 1 st at beg of next row, then at same edge every row 7 times more—62 (69) sts. Knit next row for turning ridge. Change to larger needles and A. Work even in St st for 0 (6) rows. Cont in St st and work chart I, beg and end as indicated. Work through row 20 (14). Mark end of last row for beg of pocket opening. Work through row 48 (42). Mark end of last row for end of pocket openings. Work through row 138.

Neck shaping

Row 139 (RS) Bind off first 7 sts, work to end. Dec 1 st at neck edge on next row, then every row 8 times more—46 (53) sts. Work through row 157. With A only, work 1 row more. Bind off. Place markers for 6 buttons along right front edge, with the first 2"/5cm from turning ridge, the last 1½"/4cm from neck edge and the others evenly spaced between.

LEFT FRONT

With smaller needles and B, cast on 54 (61) sts. Work in St st for 9 rows, inc 1 st at end of next row, then at same edge every row 7 times more—62 (69) sts. Knit next row for turning ridge. Change to larger needles and A. Work even in St st for 0 (6) rows. Cont in St st and work chart I, beg and end as indicated. AT THE SAME TIME, work buttonholes opposite markers on right front as foll:

Buttonhole row (RS) K to last 4 sts, k2tog, yo, k2. AT THE SAME TIME, work through row 20 (14). Mark beg of last row for beg of pocket opening. Work through row 48 (42). Mark beg of last row for end of pocket openings. Work through row 139.

Neck shaping

Row 140 (WS) Bind off first 7 sts, work to end. Cont to work as for right front, reversing all shaping.

SLEEVES

With smaller needles and B, cast on 50 (54) sts. Work in St st for 7 rows. Knit next row for turning ridge. Change to larger needles. Cont in St st and work chart II, beg and end as indicated. AT THE SAME TIME, inc 1 st each side every 3rd row 0 (7) times, every 4th row 25 (20) times—100 (108) sts. Work even through row 104. Bind off.

FINISHING

Block pieces to measurements.

Pockets

With RS facing, larger needles and A, pick up and k 20 sts evenly spaced along back right edge between pocket markers. Beg with a p row, work in St st for 4½"/11.5cm. Bind off. Rep on opposite edge of back and on each front. Sew shoulder seams.

Button band

With RS facing, smaller circular needle and B, pick up and k 122 (127) sts evenly spaced along right front edge. Work back and forth using 2nd circular needle. Knit next row for turning ridge. Work in St st for 9 rows, dec 1 st at beg of next row, then at same edge every row 7 times more. Bind off all sts loosely.

Buttonhole band

With RS facing, smaller circular needle and B, pick up and k 122 (127) sts evenly spaced along left front edge. Knit next row for turning ridge. Work in St st for 9 rows, dec 1 st at end of next row, then at same edge every row 7 times more. AT THE SAME TIME, when 4 rows of St st have been completed, work another 6 buttonholes to match previous buttonholes. Bind off all sts loosely.

Collar

With RS facing, smaller needles and B, pick up and k 82 sts evenly spaced along neck edge, beg 1"/2.5cm from right front edge and ending 1"/2.5cm from left front edge. Work even in garter st for 4 (4½)"/10 (11.5)cm. Bind off all sts loosely knitwise. Place markers 11 (12)"/28 (30.5)cm down from shoulders on back and fronts. Sew sleeves to armholes between markers. Sew side, pocket, and sleeve seams. Turn front and bottom bands to WS along turning ridges and hem in place, sewing mitered corner edges together. Turn sleeve bands to WS along turning ridges and hem in place. Sew on buttons.

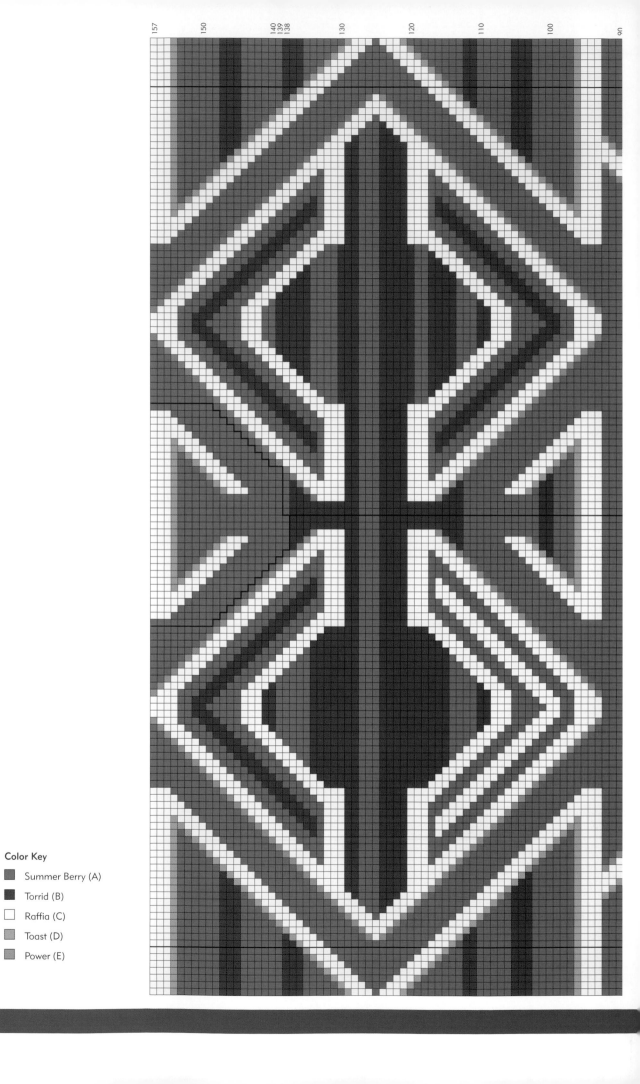

Color Key

- ■ Summer Berry (A)
- ■ Torrid (B)
- □ Raffia (C)
- ■ Toast (D)
- ■ Power (E)

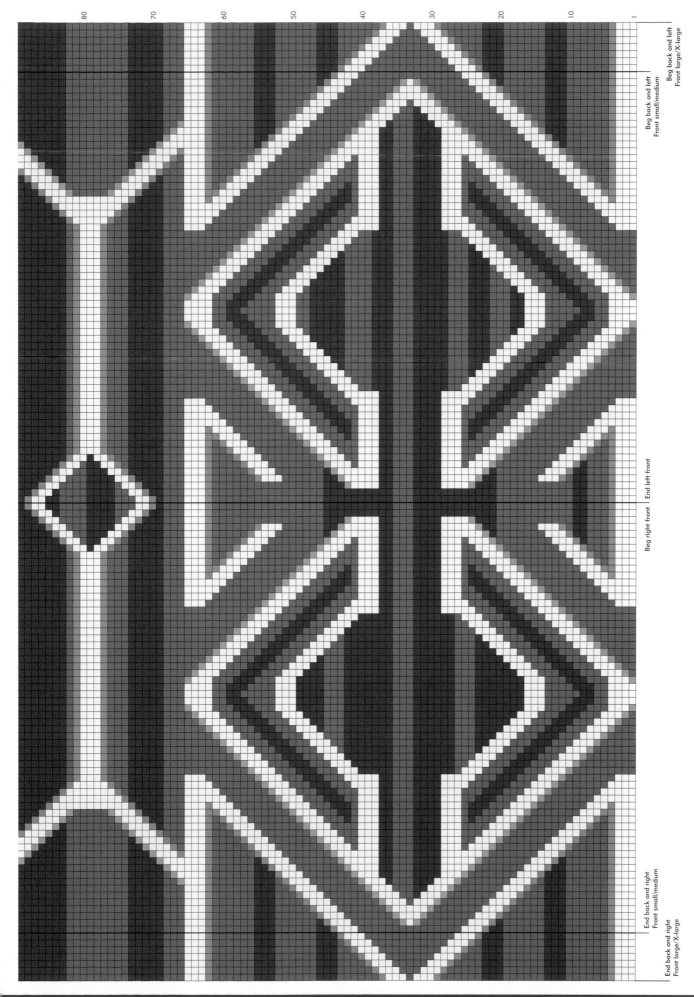

End small/medium

End large/X-large

Beg small/medium

Beg large/X-large

20

10

1

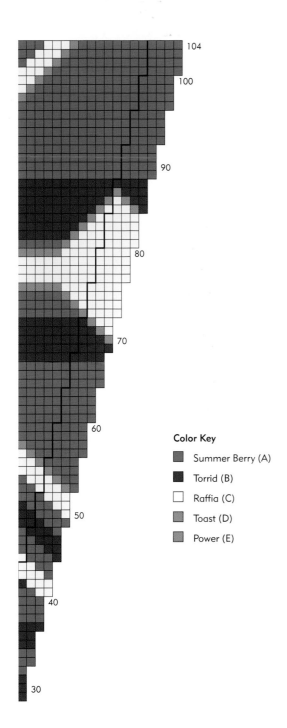

104

100

90

80

70

60

Color Key

■ Summer Berry (A)

■ Torrid (B)

□ Raffia (C)

■ Toast (D)

■ Power (E)

50

40

30

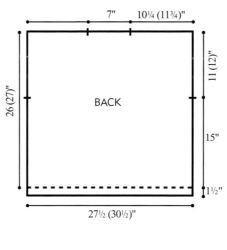

7"   10¼ (11¾)"

11 (12)"

26 (27)"   BACK

15"

1½"

27½ (30½)"

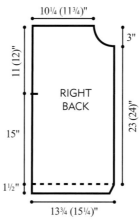

10¼ (11¾)"

11 (12)"   3"

RIGHT
BACK   23 (24)"

15"

1½"

13¾ (15¼)"

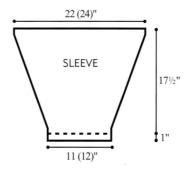

22 (24)"

SLEEVE   17½"

1"

11 (12)"

Harvest Vest

Materials

Colorway I

■ 2 (2, 3) 1¾oz/50g hanks (each approx 118yd/108m) of Rowan Yarns Summer Tweed (cotton) in #522 smoulder (E)

■ 1 (1, 2) hank each in #507 rush (A), #509 sunset (B), #510 bouquet (C), #514 reed (D), #523 legend (F), and #529 denim (G)

Colorway II

■ 2 hanks in #514 reed (E)

■ 1 hank each in #537 summer berry (A), #536 torrid (B), #539 vanity (C), #523 legend (D), #529 denim (F), and #530 toast (G)

■ One pair each sizes 7 and 8 (4.5 and 5mm) needles OR SIZE TO OBTAIN GAUGE

■ Size 7 (4.5mm) circular needle, 24"/60cm long

■ Bobbins

■ Stitch holders

Sizes

Instructions are written for size Small. Changes for Medium and Large are in parentheses.

Finished Measurements

■ Bust (closed) 38 (42, 47)"/96.5 (106.5, 119)cm

■ Length 20 (21, 22)"/51 (53.5, 56)cm

Gauge

27 sts to 8"/20.5cm and 22 rows to 4"/10cm over St st and chart pat using larger needles.

TAKE TIME TO CHECK YOUR GAUGE.

Notes

1 Do not carry colors across; use a separate bobbin of color for each color section.

2 When changing colors, pick up new color from under dropped color to prevent holes.

3 Keep color changes on WS side of work.

BACK

With smaller needles and E, cast on 65 (71, 79) sts. Work in St st for 5 rows. Knit next row for turning ridge. Change to larger needles. Cont in St st and work chart 1, beg and end as indicated. Work through row 19, then rep rows 6-19 until piece measures 12 (12½,13)"/30.5 (31.5, 33)cm from turning ridge, end with a WS row.

Armhole shaping

Bind off 5 sts at beg of next 2 rows. Dec 1 st each side every row 5 times, then every other row 3 times—39 (45, 53) sts. Work even until armhole measures 7 (7½, 8)"/17.5 (19, 20.5)cm, end with a WS row.

Shoulder shaping

Bind off 5 (7, 8) sts at beg of next 2 rows, then 6 (7, 9) sts at beg of next 2 rows. Place rem 17 (17, 19) sts on holder for back neck.

LEFT FRONT

With smaller needles and E, cast on 32 (35, 39) sts. Work in St st for 5 rows. Knit next row for turning ridge. Change to larger needles. Cont in St st and work chart 2, beg and end as indicated. Work through row 19, then rep rows 6-19 until piece measures same length as back to armhole, end with a WS row.

Neck and armhole shaping

Dec 1 st at neck edge on next row, then every 4th row 7 (7, 8) times more. AT SAME TIME, shape armhole at side edge as for back. Work even on 11 (14, 17) sts until piece measures same length as back to shoulder, end with a WS row. Shape shoulder at side edge as for back.

RIGHT FRONT

With smaller needles and E, cast on 32 (35, 39) sts. Work in St st for 5 rows. Knit next row for turning ridge. Change to larger needles. Cont in

St st and work chart 3, beg and end as indicated. Cont to work as for left front, reversing all shaping.

FINISHING

Block pieces to measurements. Sew shoulder seams.

Neckband

With RS facing, circular needle and E, pick up and k 81 (85, 88) sts along right front from turning ridge to shoulder seam, k 17 (17, 19) sts from back neck holder inc 1 st in center, pick up and k 81 (85, 88) sts along left front from shoulder seam to turning ridge—180 (188, 196) sts. Do not join. Purl next row. Cont in St st and block pat as folls: **Row 1 (RS)** *K4 with A, k4 with G, k4 with D, k4 with F, k4 with B, k4 with G, k4 with C, k4 with E, k4 with F; rep from * 4 times more. **For size Medium only** End k4 with A, k4 with G. **For size Large only** End k4 with A, k4 with G, k4 with D, k4 with F. **For all sizes** Cont to work in St st as established for 3 more rows. With E only, p next 2 rows for turning ridge. Cont in St st for 4 rows. Bind off all sts loosely.

Armbands

With RS facing, smaller needles and E, pick up and k 76 (80, 84) sts evenly spaced along armhole edge. Purl next row. Cont in St st and block pat as folls: **Row 1 (RS)** *K4 with A, k4 with G, k4 with D, k4 with F, k4 with B, k4 with G, k4 with C, k4 with E, k4 with F; rep from * once more. **For size Small only** End k4 with A. **For size Medium only** End k4 with A, k4 with G. **For size Large only** End k4 with A, k4 with G, k4 with D. **For all sizes** Cont to work as established for 3 more rows. With E only, p next 2 rows for turning ridge. Cont in St st for 4 rows. Bind off all sts loosely. Sew side and armband seams. Turn each band to WS along turning ridge and hem in place.

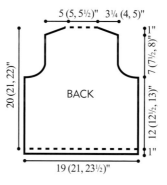

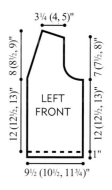

Vogue Knitting had invited me to join them on a cruise to Alaska to teach knitting workshops. Discovering firsthand this land of frozen landscapes, ice-covered mountainsides, and summers without night was very intriguing.

Leaving the skyscrapers of Vancouver, Canada, I boarded the pristine *Sea Princess* cruise liner with its tiny black portholes studding the ship's side like a neat row of buttons on a tuxedo shirt. Colorful crates of fruits and vegetables were hauled aboard by cranes as we readied for the journey ahead of us.

Leaving port, the ship glided through the steely blue-gray waters. Each morning I pulled back my cabin curtains to reveal towering, deep-blue, crag-

gy mountains falling to sea level where the small towns we visited—Ketchikan, Skagway, Juneau, and others—were tucked away. Tiny water planes flew in and out of the ports like mosquitoes. From the ship's balcony I admired, with great curiosity, the life of these towns and their people. I can remember like yesterday taking a helicopter flight over a glacier. I was staggered by the scale of the vast ice floe filling the open valley high up in the mountains. It felt surreal, as if we were on the moon. The ice resembled a mass of wallpaper paste, reflecting shades of pale cream, pink, and light gray, with luminous turquoise-blue crevices.

I have returned several times to this curious land—once in the heart of winter to see how much snow Alaska really has, and how I'd cope with it (I loved it!). I was brave enough to take a snow bath to celebrate. I stayed in a wooden lodge on the edge of frozen Finger Lake, an hour's plane ride from Anchorage. This is one of the stopping points for the world-famous Iditarod dog race.

The only lifeline to this lodge was a tiny snow plane that acted as the passenger transport, garbage truck, and food carrier. When we flew over the snow-packed landscape, the only definition on the ground

From left to right: Mushing with the huskies in Alaska; the overwhelming scale and subtle coloration of the frozen landscape; mysteriously rich mossy green textures on the shore of a lake.

below was the primitive pencil sketch of the frozen river between the bare, wispy trees. Occasionally, we would see moose plodding through the snow. (My diary of this adventure can be read at my Web site, www.brandonmably.com.)

The landscape was dramatically beautiful, with constantly changing and moving weather fronts. The blinding sun glared off the snow and the wide-open frozen lake was like an enormous ice-skating rink. This expanse reached toward the walls of the distant mountains, pink and

yellow pastels in the early morning, powder-blue and cold gray in the evening light. This was no white wonderland; the snow reflected all the colors of the sky. Combining the palette from the wilderness with the pattern of the rippling waves on the water, I came up with this design for a fresh two-color-per-row garment using the gorgeous Rowan Summer Tweed range. If you're not comfortable in light colors, try replacing the cream background with a warm brown—it should be rather handsome.

From left to right: Blue and white stripes grace the deck of a cruise ship; the tonal colors of the huskies against the winter landscape; admiring the turquoise hues inside a glacier's crevice.

Glacier Jacket

Materials

- 6 (6, 7) 1oz/50g ball (each approx 117yd/108m) of Rowan Yarns Summer Tweed (cotton/silk) in #508 oats (A)

- 3 (3, 4) balls in #506 ghost (B)

- 1 ball each in #514 reed (C), #515 raffia (D), #527 sprig (E), #500 powder (F), #539 vanity (G), #525 blueberry (H), #512 exotic (J), and #536 torrid (K)

- One pair each sizes 6 and 8 (4 and 5mm) needles OR SIZE TO OBTAIN GAUGE

- Six ½"/13mm buttons and bobbins

Sizes

Sized for Small/Medium, Large/X-Large, 2X/3X. Shown in size Large/X-Large.

Finished Measurements

- Bust (buttoned) 39 (48, 56)"/100 (122, 142)cm

- Length 23 (23, 24)"/58.5 (58.5, 61)cm

- Upper arm 16 (17, 19)"/40.5 (44.5, 48.5)cm

Gauge

18 sts and 26 rows to 4"/10cm over St st and chart pat using larger needles.

TAKE TIME TO CHECK YOUR GAUGE.

Notes

When changing colors in chart pat, twist yarns on WS to prevent holes in work. Wind colors onto bobbins. Work each block of color with a separate bobbin.

BACK

With smaller needles and B, cast on 88 (110, 132) sts. Work in garter st for 4 rows. Change to larger needles and A. Work in St st for 2 (2, 6) rows. Cont in St st as foll:

Beg chart pat

Row 1 (RS) Work 22-st rep of chart (page 153) 4 (5, 6) times. Cont in this way until 72 rows of chart have been worked twice. Work 0 (0, 4) rows with A. Piece measures approx 23 (23, 24)"/58.5 (58.5, 61)cm from beg. Bind off all sts.

LEFT FRONT

With smaller needles and B, cast on 44 (52, 60) sts. Work in garter st for 4 rows. Change to larger needles and A. Work in St st for 2 (2, 6) rows.

Beg chart pat

Row 1 (RS) K0 (4, 8), work 22-st rep of chart twice, k0 (4, 8). Cont in this way, keeping first and last 0 (4, 8) sts matching colors on chart until 72 rows of chart have been worked once, then work rows 1-53 once. Piece measures approx 20¼ (20¼, 20¾)"/51.5 (51.5, 52.5)cm from beg.

Neck shaping

Neck row (WS) Bind off 2 sts (neck edge), work to end. Cont to dec 1 st at neck edge every row 13 (10, 8) times—29 (40, 50) sts. Work even until same length as back. Bind off rem sts for shoulder.

RIGHT FRONT

Work to correspond to left front, reversing neck shaping.

SLEEVES

With smaller needles and B, cast on 44 sts. Work in garter st for 4 rows. Change to larger needles and A and work in St st for 2 rows.

Beg chart pat

Row 1 (RS) Work 22-st rep of chart twice. Cont in this way, inc 1 st each side (working inc sts into chart pat) every 8th (6th, 4th) row 14 (18, 8) times, then every 0 (0, 6th) row 0 (0, 13) times—72 (80, 86) sts. Work even until 72 rows of chart have been worked once, then work rows 1–44 once more—piece measures approx 19"/48cm from beg. Bind off.

FINISHING

Sew shoulder seams.

Button band

With RS facing, smaller needles and A, beg just below neck shaping, pick up and k 91 sts evenly along left front edge. Work in garter st for 3 rows. Bind off.

Buttonhole band

With RS facing, smaller needles and A, beg at lower edge, pick up and k 91 (91, 93) sts evenly along right front edge up to neck shaping. K 1 row.

Next (buttonhole) row (RS) K4 (4, 5), k2tog, yo, [k18, k2tog, yo] 4 times, k to end. K 1 row. Bind off.

Neckband

With RS facing, smaller needles and A, beg at edge of buttonhole band, pick up and k 22 sts along right front neck, 31 (31, 33) sts along back neck and 22 sts along left front neck—75 (75, 77) sts. K 1 row.

Next (buttonhole) row (RS) K1, yo, k2tog, k to end. Bind off.

With center of bound-off sts of sleeves at shoulder seam, sew top of sleeve to front and back. Sew side and sleeve seams. Sew on buttons.

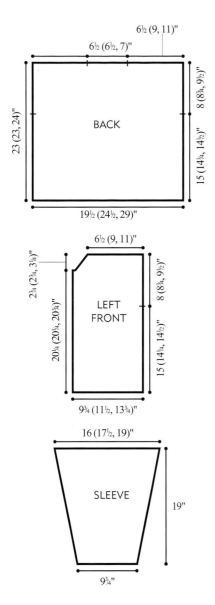

BACK

23 (23, 24)"

6½ (6½, 7)"

6½ (9, 11)"

8 (8¾, 9½)"

15 (14¼, 14½)"

19½ (24½, 29)"

LEFT FRONT

6½ (9, 11)"

2¾ (2¾, 3¼)"

20¼ (20¼, 20¾)"

8 (8¾, 9½)"

15 (14¼, 14½)"

9¾ (11½, 13¾)"

SLEEVE

16 (17½, 19)"

19"

9¾"

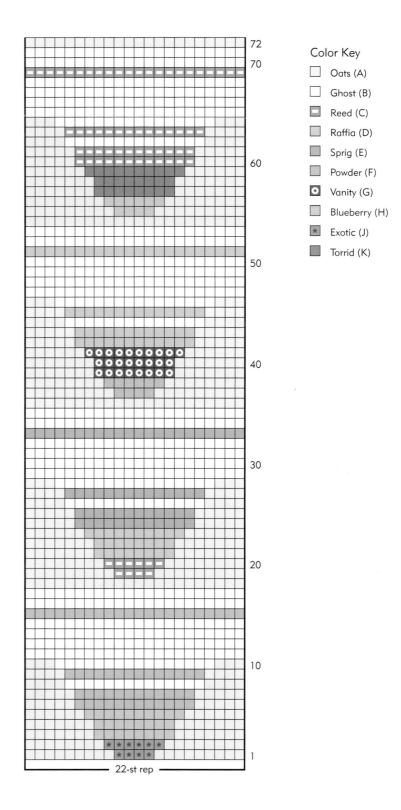

22-st rep

Color Key

☐ Oats (A)

☐ Ghost (B)

▱ Reed (C)

▨ Raffia (D)

▩ Sprig (E)

▨ Powder (F)

◉ Vanity (G)

▨ Blueberry (H)

✳ Exotic (J)

▨ Torrid (K)

Vietnam

A friend of mine invited a group of us to visit Vietnam, the land of her childhood. A few years earlier, the country had re-opened to the Western world. We were enticed by the offer and by the exquisite silk and cotton textiles she had brought back from a recent trip, along with garden ceramic pots dripping in rich glazes of deep aqua-blues, greens, and old gold.

Arriving in Vietnam from my quiet North London neighborhood was quite a culture shock. Saigon was our first port of call. The city was swarming in the humid heat with people on foot weaving their way through the thundering road traffic. We passed enchanting old villas, reminders of the country's French Colonial past. Their tall shuttered windows and wide sweeping staircases were protected by high walls. At the other extreme were the makeshift homes with roofs of rusty corrugated

iron or plastic sheeting. The street restaurants were simple: a little table, plastic stools, and a hot plate. They seemed constantly busy.

The roads were a river of rushing bikes, small cars belching exhaust, and honking horns. Crossing the road was always an alarming prospect, as the flow of cars never stopped. I observed an old lady who walked calmly into the traffic—which then passed around her like a rock in a river. It was a real test of one's nerves to follow her, but there was no other way to cross. An elegant note amid this chaos was the schoolgirls cycling along in sleek white uniforms and gloves,

Clockwise from left: Spices stacked high; beans in colored bowls; carved-out rice fields in the steep hillsides of Vietnam.

straight-backed, immaculate, and unfazed, like swans gliding through the traffic.

The marketplaces were organized intriguingly by profession: plumbers, mechanics, wood workers, etc. On one street we found plastic buckets and trays containing tools, nuts, and bolts neatly laid out; around the corner stalls sold plastic flowers, bamboo ladders, and stone carvings. When rain fell, the streets were transformed into a ballet of floating flowers. Everyone on bicycles donned pastel, plastic ponchos, gliding along like large petunias in their conical straw hats. When the sun came out, one could see how practical these hats were, providing protection in all weather. The fresh-produce market stalls were alive with inspiration—richly colored wild flowers in wire baskets, green vegetables piled high, and pyramids of pristine exotic fruit balanced on tables covered with floral plastic cloths.

Towering rock structures protruded from the deep jade-green waters on Halong Bay. Weathered gray, tan, and black clumps of foliage still managed to cling to these formidable places. Small fishing boats would sidle up beside us on the quay to sell their fresh catch. A small piece of weaving I found in the market made me think of these imposing island structures. I was inspired to translate the idea into the pillows presented in this chapter. One colorway is knitted with a tweedy green back-ground; the other in tweedy rust from the Rowan

Scottish yarn range. It is fascinating to see how a different background changes the look.

In Vietnam, every inch of available land is farmed. Rice fields are dug into the steepest hillsides, forming a pattern resembling empty bookshelves. I've translated this idea into a neat vest using 4-ply yarn, a design I'm rather pleased with.

From left to right: Handmade wicker containers; brocade umbrellas blending into a lichen-covered tree; a lake brimming with lily pads.

Steps Vest

Materials

- 4 (4, 5) .87oz/25g balls (each approx 120yd/110m) of Rowan Yarns Yorkshire Tweed 4 Ply (wool) in #286 graze (E)
- 4 (4, 5) .87oz/25g balls (each approx 120yd/110m) of Rowan Yarns Scottish Tweed 4 Ply (wool) in #18 thatch (D)
- 3 (3, 4) balls each in #19 peat (A) and #15 apple (B)
- 2 balls in #22 celtic mix (C)
- One pair each sizes 2 and 3 (2.75 and 3.25mm) needles OR SIZE TO OBTAIN GAUGE
- Two size 2 (2.75mm) circular needles, 24"/60cm long
- Bobbins
- Stitch holder
- Seven ⅝"/16mm buttons

Sizes

Instructions are written for men's size Small. Changes for Medium and Large are in parentheses.

Finished Measurements

- Chest 42 (45, 48)"/106.5 (114.5, 122)cm
- Length 25½ (26, 26½)"/64.5 (66, 67.5)cm

Gauge

28 sts and 40 rows to 4"/10cm over St st and chart pat using larger needles.

TAKE TIME TO CHECK YOUR GAUGE.

Notes

1 Do not carry colors across, use a separate bobbin of color for each color section.

2 When changing colors, pick up new color from under dropped color to prevent holes.

3 Keep color changes on WS side of work.

BACK

With smaller needles and A, cast on 148 (158, 168) sts. Work in St st for 11 rows. Knit next row for turning ridge. Cont in St st for 2 more rows.

Beg chart pat 1

Row 1 (RS) Beg with st 15 (10, 5), work to end of 44-st rep, work sts 23-66 twice, then work sts 67-74 (67-79, 67-84) once. Cont to foll chart in this way through row 10. Change to larger needles.

Beg chart pat 2

Cont in St st and work chart, beg and end as indicated. Work through row 166.

Armhole shaping

Bind off 6 (7, 8) sts at beg of next 2 rows, 5 (6, 7) sts at beg of next 2 rows, then 2 sts at beg of next 8 rows. Dec 1 st each side every row 12 (13, 13) times, then every 4th row twice—82 (86, 92) sts. Work even through row 242 (246, 250).

Shoulder shaping

With B, bind off 23 (24, 26) sts at beg of next 2 rows. Place rem 36 (38, 40) sts on holder for back neck.

LEFT FRONT

With smaller needles and A, cast on 74 (79, 84) sts. Work in St st for 11 rows. Knit next row for turning ridge. Cont in St st for 2 more rows.

Beg chart pat 1

Row 1 (RS) Beg with st 15 (10, 5), then work to st 88. Cont to foll chart in this way through row 10. Change to larger needles.

Beg chart pat 2

Cont in St st and work chart, beg and end as indicated. Work through row 166.

Neck and armhole shaping

Row 167 (RS) Bind off 6 (7, 8) sts, work to last 2 sts, k2tog. Cont to dec 1 st from neck edge every 6th row twice more, every 4th row 13 times, then every 3rd row 2 (3, 4) times. AT THE SAME TIME, cont to bind off 5 (6, 7) sts from armhole edge once, then 2 sts 4 times. Dec 1 st from armhole edge every row 12 (13, 13) times, then every 4th row twice. Work even on 23 (24, 26) sts through row 242 (246, 250). With B, bind off all sts.

RIGHT FRONT

With smaller needles and A, cast on 74 (79, 84) sts. Work in St st for 11 rows. Knit next row for turning ridge. Cont in St st for 2 more rows.

Beg chart pat 1

Row 1 (RS) Beg with st 1, then work to st 74 (79, 84). Cont to foll chart in this way through row 10. Change to larger needles.

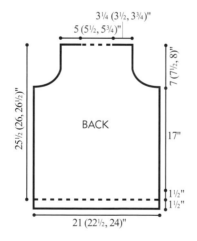

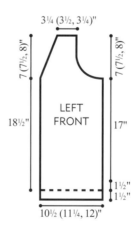

Beg chart pat 2

Cont in St st and work chart, beg and end as indicated. Work through row 166.

Neck and armhole shaping

Row 167 (RS) K2tog, work to end.

Row 168 (WS) Bind off 6 (7, 8) sts, work to end. Cont to work as for left front, reversing all shaping.

FINISHING

Block pieces to measurements. Sew shoulder seams. Turn bottom band to WS along turning ridge and hem in place. On each front, place a yarn marker at beg of neck shaping. Place markers for 7 buttonholes along left front edge, with the first 1"/2.5cm from lower edge, the last at beg of neck shaping and the others evenly spaced between.

Neckband

With RS facing, circular needle and A, pick up and k 132 sts evenly spaced along right front edge to beg of neck shaping, 53 (56, 59) sts to right shoulder, k 36 (38, 40) sts from back neck holder, pick up and k 53 (56, 59) sts to beg of left neck shaping, then 132 sts along left front edge—406 (414, 422) sts. Work back and forth using 2nd circular needle.

Beg chart pat 1

Beg with a p row (WS) and working chart from left to right, cont in St st as folls:

Row 2 (WS) Beg with st 71 (75, 79), work to end of 44-st rep, work sts 66-23 8 times, then work sts 22-18 (22-14, 22-10) once. Cont to foll chart in this way through row 4. Row 5 (RS) Work buttonholes at markers as folls: *work to marker, yo, k2tog; rep from * 6 times more. Cont to foll chart through row 9. With A only, p next 2 rows for turning ridge. Beg with a p row, cont in St st for 4 rows. Work buttonhole row once more. Cont in St st for 4 more rows. Bind off all sts loosely purlwise.

Armbands

With RS facing, smaller needles and A, pick up and k 116 (126, 136) sts evenly spaced along armhole edge.

Beg chart pat 1

Beg with a p row (WS) and working chart from left to right, cont in St st as folls:

Row 2 (WS) Beg with st 80 (85, 68), work to end of 44-st rep, work sts 66-23 1 (1, 2) times, then work sts 22-9 (22-4, 22-21) once. Cont to foll chart in this way through row 5. With A only, p next 2 rows for turning ridge. Beg with a p row, cont in St st for 5 rows. Bind off all sts loosely purlwise. Sew side and armband seams. Turn each band to WS along turning ridge and hem in place. Sew on buttons.

Body Chart Bottom

chart pat 2

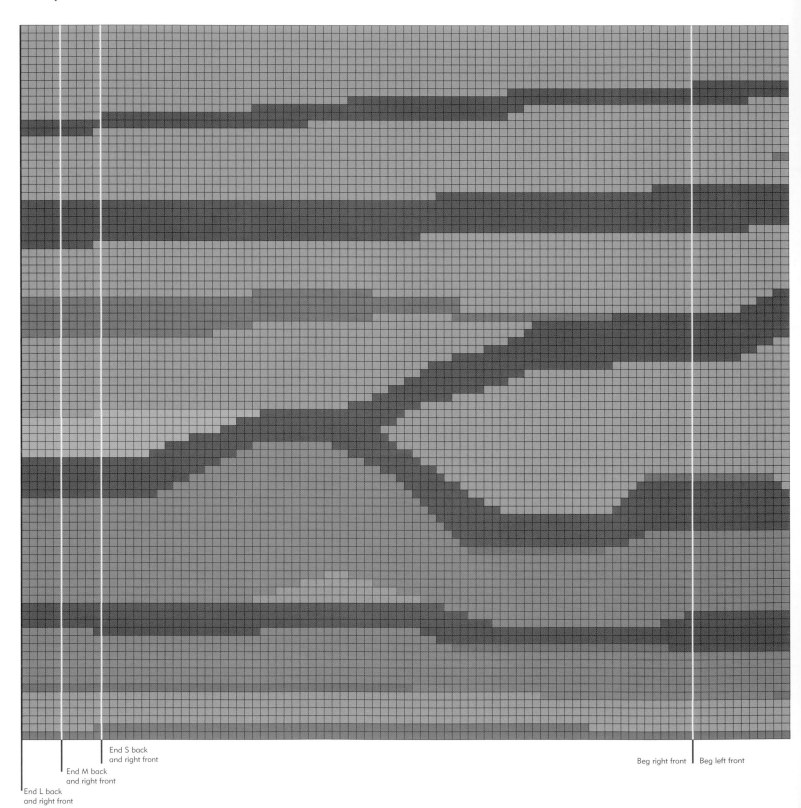

End S back
and right front

End M back
and right front

End L back
and right front

Beg right front Beg left front

chart pat 1

44-st rep

10
9
7
5
3
1

88 87 85 83 81 79 77 75 73 71 69 67 65 63 61 59 57 55 53 51 49 47 45 43 41 39 37 35 33 31 29 27 25 23 21 19 17 15 13 11 9 7 5 3 1

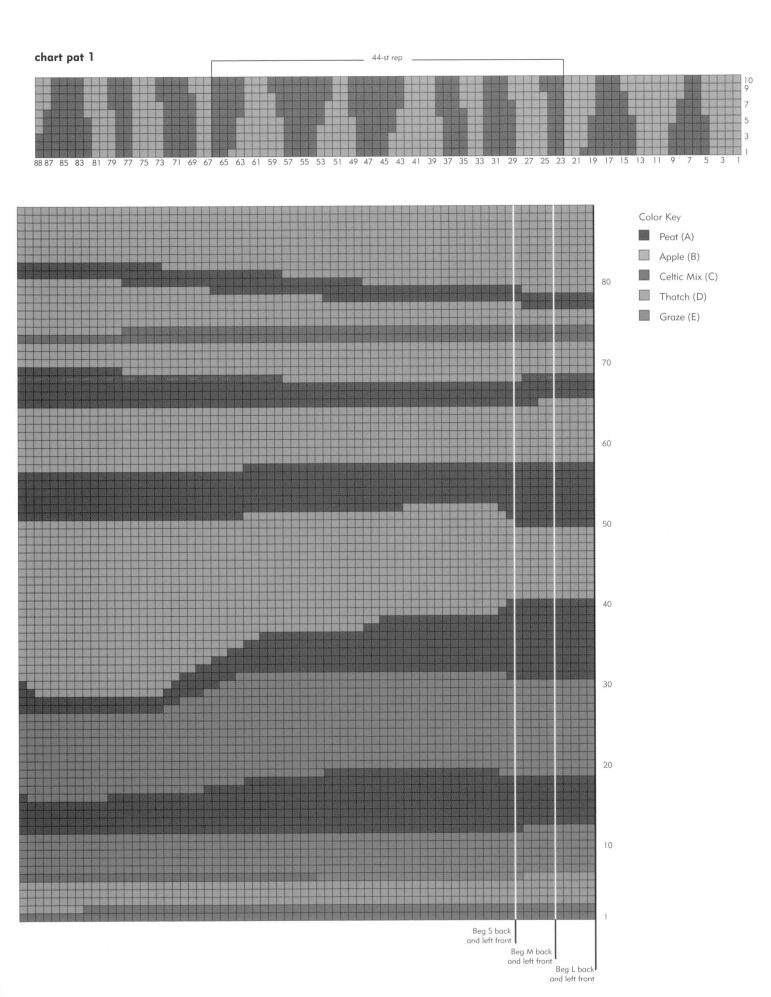

Color Key

■ Peat (A)
■ Apple (B)
■ Celtic Mix (C)
■ Thatch (D)
■ Graze (E)

80

70

60

50

40

30

20

10

1

Beg S back
and left front

Beg M back
and left front

Beg L back
and left front

chart pat 2

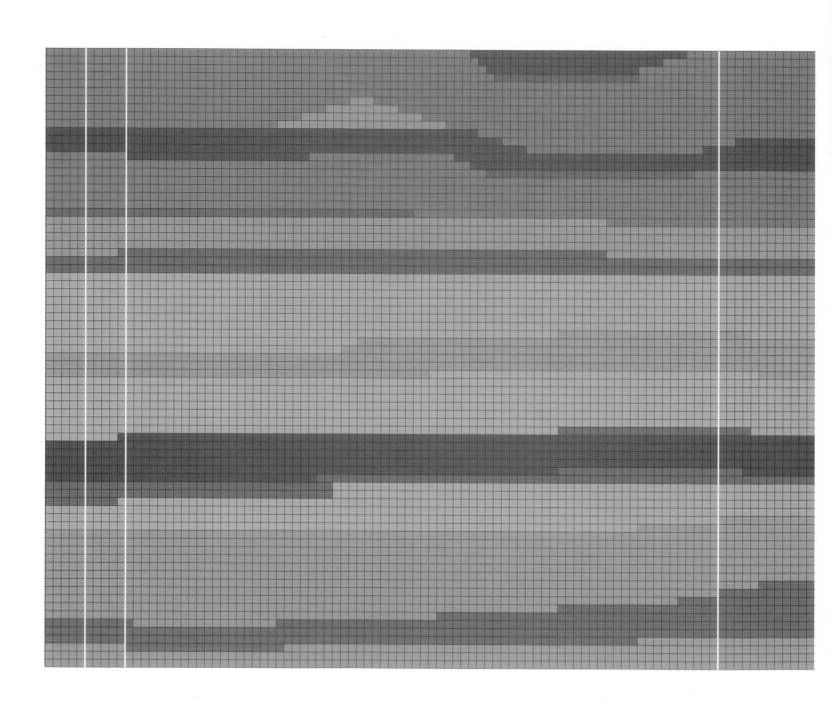

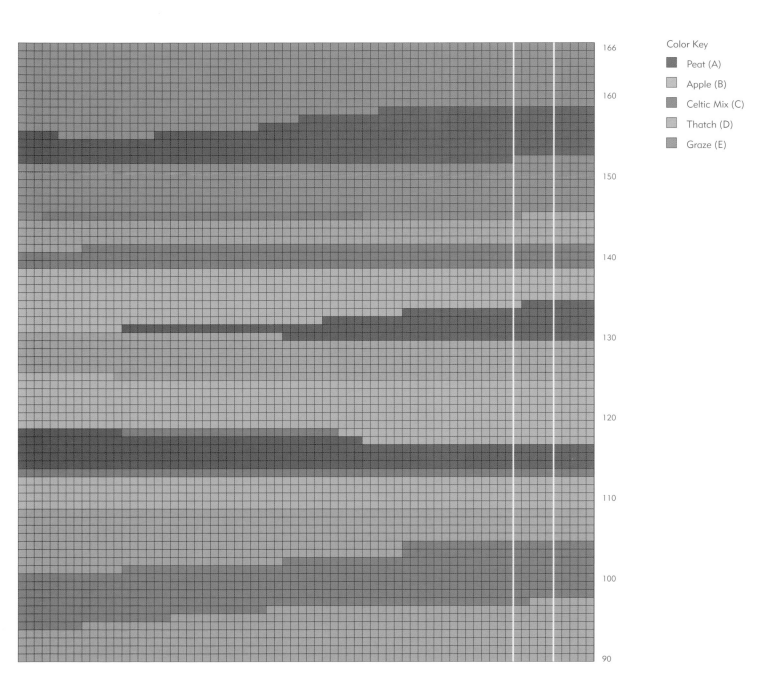

Color Key

■ Peat (A)
■ Apple (B)
■ Celtic Mix (C)
■ Thatch (D)
■ Graze (E)

166
160
150
140
130
120
110
100
90

Body Chart Top

chart pat 2

Color Key
- Peat (A)
- Apple (B)
- Celtic Mix (C)
- Thatch (D)
- Graze (E)

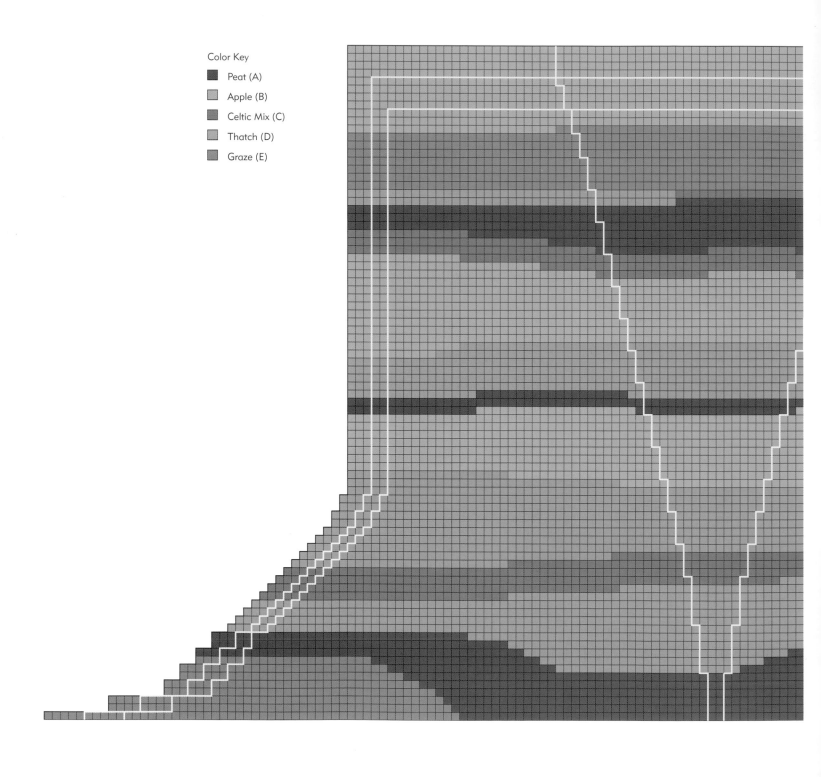

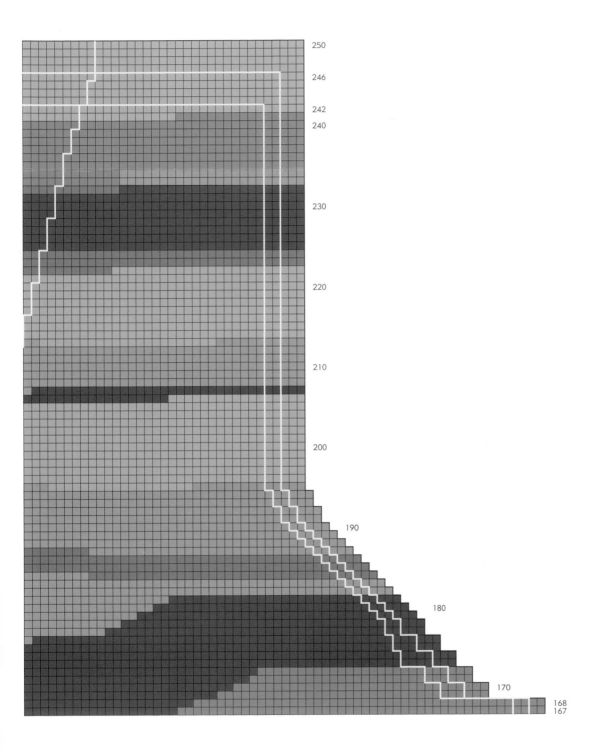

250

246

242
240

230

220

210

200

190

180

170

168
167

Island Pillows

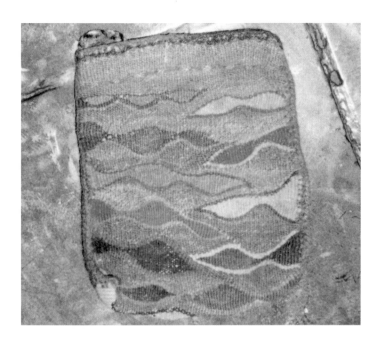

Materials

Colorway I

- 2 .87oz/25g balls (each approx 120yd/110m) of Rowan Yarns Yorkshire Tweed 4 Ply (wool) in #273 glory (A)

- 1 ball each in #271 cheerful (B), #274 brilliant (C), and #286 graze (D)

- 1 .87oz/25g ball (each approx 120yd/110m) of Rowan Yarns Scottish Tweed 4 Ply (wool) in #11 sunset (E)

Colorway II

- 2 .87oz/25g balls (each approx 120yd/110m) of Rowan Yarns Yorkshire Tweed 4 Ply (wool) in #286 graze (A)

- 1 ball each in #271 cheerful (B), #274 brilliant (C), and #273 glory (D)

- 1 .87oz/25g ball (each approx 120yd/110m) of Rowan Yarns Scottish Tweed 4 Ply (wool) in #11 sunset (E)

- One pair size 6 (4mm) needles OR SIZE TO OBTAIN GAUGE

- Bobbins

- Four ¾"/19mm buttons

- 15" x 15"/38 x 38cm pillow form

Finished Measurements

- 15" x 15"/38 x 38cm

Gauge

20 sts and 28 rows to 4"/10cm over St st and chart pat using size 6 (4mm) needles and 2 strands held tog.

TAKE TIME TO CHECK YOUR GAUGE.

Notes

1 Use 2 strands of yarn held tog throughout.

2 When working rows 1–4 and 81–84, you may carry color not in use loosely across WS of work.

3 For all other rows, do not carry colors across. Use a separate bobbin of color for each color section.

4 When changing colors, pick up new color from under dropped color to prevent holes.

5 Keep color changes on WS side of work.

SEED STITCH

Row 1 *K1, p1; rep from * to end.

Row 2 Knit the p sts and purl the k sts.

Rep row 2 for seed st.

FRONT

With 2 strands of A held tog, cast on 80 sts. Work in St st for 6 rows. Cont in St st and work rows 1–84 of chart. With A only, work in St st for 6 rows. Bind off.

BACK

Bottom half

With 2 strands of A held tog, cast on 80 sts. Cont in St st and stripe pat as folls: 4 rows A, 1 row C, 3 rows E, 4 rows A, 5 rows B, 3 rows D, 2 rows A, 3 rows C, 5 rows E, 2 rows A, 1 row B, 2 rows D, 5 rows A, 3 rows C and 2 rows E. Cont with A only as folls:

Button band

Work in seed st for 12 rows. Bind off all sts loosely in seed st. Place markers for 4 buttons on button band, with the first and last 2½"/6.5cm from side edges and the others evenly spaced between.

Top half

Work as for bottom half to button band. Cont with A only as folls:

Buttonhole band

Work in seed st for 6 rows.

Buttonhole row (RS) *Work in seed st to marker, yo, k2tog; rep from * 3 times more, work in seed st to end. Cont in seed st for 5 more rows. Bind off all sts loosely in seed st.

FINISHING

Block pieces to measurements. Lap back buttonhole band over button band; pin together along length of bands. With RS facing, sew front and back together around all edges. Remove pins. Turn RS out. Sew on buttons to correspond to buttonholes. Insert pillow form; button closed.

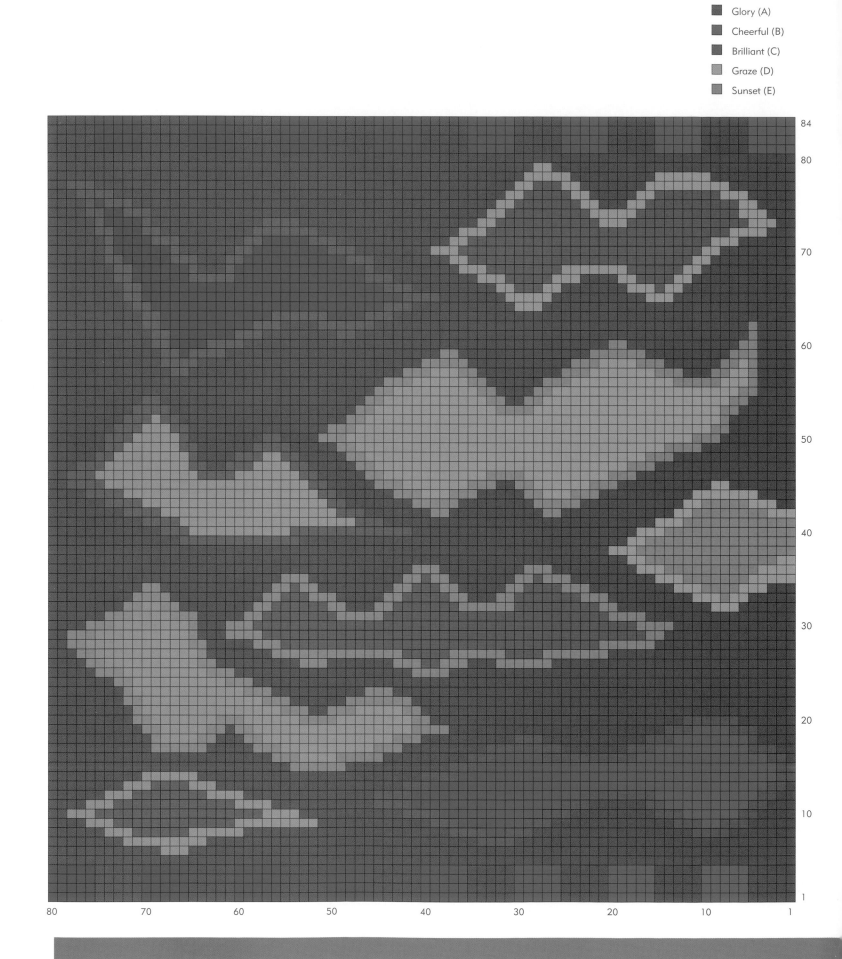

Color Key
Glory (A)
Cheerful (B)
Brilliant (C)
Graze (D)
Sunset (E)

Colorway II

Color Key

■ Graze (A)
■ Cheerful (B)
■ Brilliant (C)
■ Glory (D)
■ Sunset (E)

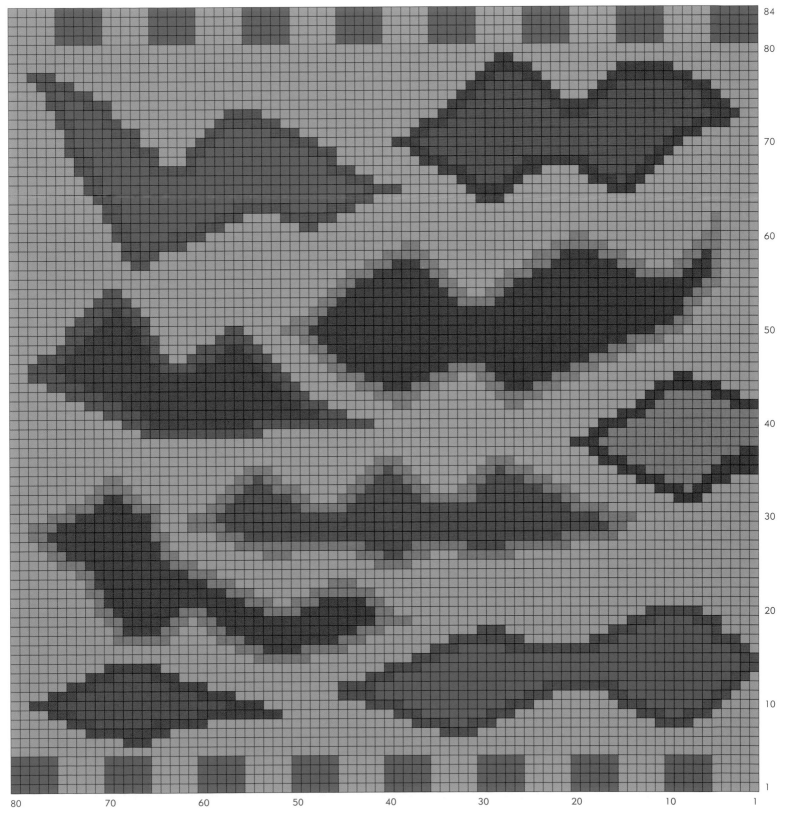

Technical Instructions

Many of the patterns in this book look very complex—which may lead you to believe that they are difficult to knit. In fact, they are not hard at all. They rely mostly on stockinette stitch and ribbing, with the occasional edging in crochet, moss stitch, or garter stitch. The simple stitches free you up to concentrate on the color.

Fair Isle Knitting

Stranding – One-handed

1. On the knit side, drop the working yarn. Bring the new color (now the working yarn) over the top of the dropped yarn and work to the next color change.

2. Drop the working yarn. Bring the new color under the dropped yarn and work to the next color change. Repeat steps 1 and 2.

1. On the purl side, drop the working yarn. Bring the new color (now the working yarn) over the top of the dropped yarn and work to the next color change.

2. Drop the working yarn. Bring the new color under the dropped yarn and work to the next color change. Repeat steps 1 and 2.

Stranding – Two-handed

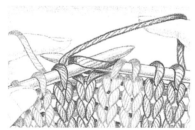   

1. On the knit side, hold the working yarn in your right hand and the non-working yarn in your left hand. Bring the working yarn over the top of the yarn in your left hand and knit with the right hand to the next color change.

2. The yarn in your right hand is now the non-working yarn; the yarn in your left hand is the working yarn. Bring the working yarn under the non-working yarn and knit with the left hand to the next color change. Repeat steps 1 and 2.

1. On the purl side, hold the working yarn in your right hand and the non-working yarn in your left hand. Bring the working yarn over the top of the yarn in your left hand and purl with the right hand to the next color change.

2. The yarn in your right hand is now the non-working yarn; the yarn in your left hand is the working yarn. Bring the working yarn under the non-working yarn and purl with the left hand to the next color change. Repeat steps 1 and 2.

Handling a large number of colors sometimes worries knitters, but it's not as difficult as it seems. The most important thing to do when knitting with lots of colors is to handle the yarns properly. There are two main methods: Fair isle and Intarsia.

Weaving

1. Hold the working yarn in your right hand and the yarn to be woven in your left. To weave the yarn above a knit stitch, bring it over the right needle. Knit the stitch with the working yarn, bringing it under the woven yarn.

2. The woven yarn will go under the next knit stitch. With the working yarn, knit the stitch, bringing the yarn over the woven yarn. Repeat steps 1 and 2 to the next color change.

1. To weave the yarn above a purl stitch, bring it over the right needle. Purl the stitch with the working yarn, bringing it under the woven yarn.

2. To weave the yarn below a purl stitch, purl the stitch with the working yarn, bringing it over the woven yarn. Repeats steps 1 and 2 to the next color change.

Twisting

On the knit side, twist the working yarn and the carried yarn around each other once. Then continue with the same color as before.

On the purl side, twist the yarns around each other as shown, then continue purling with the same color as before.

Intarsia

Intarsia is a colorwork technique in which blocks of color are worked with separate balls of yarn or bobbins. The yarns are not carried across the back of the work between color changes to prevent holes in the work.

Intarsia knitting should not be worked circularly because at the end of the round, the yarns would be in the wrong position. You would have to cut all the yarn and reattach it, leaving you to weave in hundreds of ends.

When changing colors in a vertical line, the yarns must be twisted on every row. When changing colors on a diagonal line, the yarns must only be twisted on every other row. If the diagonal slants to the right, twist the yarns only on knit rows. If the diagonal slants to the left, twist the yarns only on purl rows.

Changing Colors on a Vertical Line

1. On the knit side, drop the old color. Pick up the new color from under the old color and knit to the next color change.

2. On the purl side, drop the old color. Pick up the new color from under the old color and purl to the next color change. Repeat steps 1 and 2.

Changing Colors on a Diagonal Line

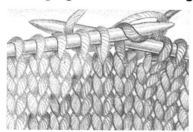   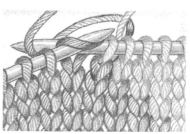

1. When working a right diagonal on the knit side, bring the new color over the top of the old color and knit to the next color change.

2. On the purl side, pick up the new color from under the old color and purl to the next color change.

1. When working a left diagonal on the purl side, bring the new color over the top of the old color and purl to the next color change.

2. On the knit side, pick up the new color from under the old color and knit to the next color change.

Backstitch

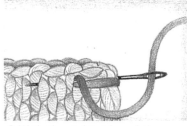 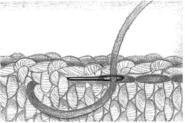

1 With the right sides of the pieces facing each other, secure the seam by taking the needle twice around the edges from back to front. Bring the needle up about one-fourth inch (.5cm) from where the yarn last emerged, as shown.

2 In one motion, insert the needle into the point where the yarn emerged from the previous stitch and back up approximately one-fourth inch (.5cm) ahead of the emerging yarn. Pull the yarn through. Repeat this step, keeping the stitches straight and even.

Vertical seam on ribbing

Knit to Knit
When joining ribbing with a knit stitch at each edge, use the bottom loop of the purl stitch on one side and the top loop of the corresponding purl stitch on the other side.

Duplicate Stitch

Duplicate stitch covers a knit stitch. Bring the needle up below the stitch to be worked. Insert the needle under both loops one row above and pull it through. Insert it back into the stitch below and through the center of the next stitch in one motion, as shown.

Terms and Abbreviations

approx approximately

beg begin(ning)

bind off Used to finish an edge and keep stitches from unraveling. Lift the first stitch over the second, the second over the third, etc. (UK: cast off)

cast on A foundation row of stitches placed on the needle in order to begin knitting.

CC contrast color

ch chain(s)

cm centimeter(s)

cn cable needle

cont continu(e)(ing)

dc double crochet (UK: tr-treble)

dec decrease(ing) — Reduce the stitches in a row (knit 2 together).

dpn double pointed needle(s)

foll follow(s)(ing)

g gram(s)

garter stitch Knit every row. Circular knitting: Knit one round, then purl one round.

hdc half-double crochet (UK: htr-half treble)

inc increase(ing) — Add stitches in a row (knit into the front and back of a stitch).

k knit

k2tog knit 2 stitches together

lp(s) loops(s)

LH left-hand

m meter(s)

M1 make one stitch — With the needle tip, lift the strand between last stitch worked and next stitch on the left-hand needle and knit into the back of it. One stitch has been added.

MC main color

mm millimeter(s)

oz ounce(s)

p purl

p2tog purl 2 stitches together

pat pattern

pick up and knit (purl) Knit (or purl) into the loops along an edge.

pm place marker — Place or attach a loop of contrast yarn or purchased stitch marker as indicated.

rem remain(s)(ing)

rep repeat

rev St st reverse Stockinette stitch — Purl right-side rows, knit wrong-side rows. Circular knitting: Purl all rounds. (UK: reverse stocking stitch)

rnd(s) round(s)

RH right-hand

RS right side(s)

sc single crochet (UK: dc - double crochet)

sk skip

SKP Slip 1, knit 1, pass slip stitch over knit 1.

SK2P Slip 1, knit 2 together, pass slip stitch over k2tog.

sl slip — An unworked stitch made by passing a stitch from the left-hand to the right-hand needle as if to purl.

sl st slip stitch (UK: single crochet)

ssk slip, slip, knit—Slip next 2 stitches knitwise, one at a time, to right-hand needle. Insert tip of left-hand needle into fronts of these stitches from left to right. Knit them together. One stitch has been decreased.

st(s) stitch(es)

St st Stockinette stitch—Knit right-side rows, purl wrong-side rows. Circular knitting: Knit all rounds. (UK: stocking stitch)

tbl through back of loop

tog together

tr treble crochet (UK: dtr-double treble)

WS wrong side(s)

w&t wrap and turn

wyif with yarn in front

wyib with yarn in back

work even Continue in pattern without increasing or decreasing. (UK: work straight)

yd yard(s)

yo yarn over—Make a new stitch by wrapping the yarn over the right-hand needle. (UK: yfwd, yon, yrn)

* Repeat directions following * as many times as indicated.

[ ] Repeat directions inside brackets as many times as indicated.

Yarn Suppliers

Westminster Fibers

4 Townsend West, Unit 8

Nashua, NH 03063

(800) 445-9276

www.knitrowan.com

Acknowledgments

The writing of this book has been an extraordinary journey; through it I've revisited in my mind all the fascinating and inspiring places I've been fortunate enough to have seen. This book wouldn't have been possible without the support and guidance of my traveling partner, friend, and mentor, Kaffe Fassett.

Behind the scenes of this production has been an army of busy hands and minds. Thanks go first to Trisha Malcolm, editorial director of Vogue Knitting, and Erica Smith of Sixth&Spring Books, for believing in me to do this book; Adina Klein for her detailed attention on the styling; and Chi Ling Moy for her gorgeous design. My utmost thanks go to Sharon Brant for her enthusiasm and support in overseeing the technical side of putting together the garments. Sincere thanks to Sharon's mother, Thelma Gardner, for finishing, along with Elaine Cockcroft, Mrs. Oaks, Audrey Barber, Wendy Shipman, and Mary Potter for their tireless hours of knitting. To all the models for making the garments look gorgeous. Thanks to Kate Buller, Colin Chawner, and Stephen Sheard at Rowan Yarns in the United Kingdom, and June and Kenneth Bridgewater in the United States, for supporting and promoting my designs, not to mention the workshop tours supported by Rowan Yarns.

I'd like to acknowledge Richard Womersley for his loyal friendship, trust, and support, Anne James for her mental stimulation, and Candace Bahouth for her loving enthusiasm and passion for creativity.

Sincere appreciation also goes to the countless friends I have made on my journeys who take the time to keep in touch from different corners of the world.

I owe a deep debt of gratitude to my good friend Sheila Rock, a London- and New York-based photographer, for producing the sumptuous images in this book.

My love and deepest appreciation goes to my mother, Yvonne, who is always quietly there for me, and my loving sisters, Eleanor and Belinda Mably. Finally, deepest thanks to my good friend Zoë Landers, who has supported me on this book every step of the way.